Global Trade and the Supply Chain

Other Books of Related Interest

Opposing Viewpoints Series
America's Infrastructure and the Green Economy
Automation of Labor
COVID-19 and the Changing Way We Live and Work
Genetically Modified Foods and the Global Food Supply

At Issue Series
Cyberwarfare
Food Security
Foreign Oil Dependence
Open Borders

Current Controversies Series
Domestic vs. Offshore Manufacturing
Fair Trade
Globalization
Tariffs and the Future of Trade

> "Congress shall make no law … abridging the freedom of speech, or of the press."
>
> *First Amendment to the U.S. Constitution*

The basic foundation of our democracy is the First Amendment guarantee of freedom of expression. The Opposing Viewpoints series is dedicated to the concept of this basic freedom and the idea that it is more important to practice it than to enshrine it.

Global Trade and the Supply Chain

Andrew Karpan, Book Editor

Published in 2023 by Greenhaven Publishing, LLC
2544 Clinton Street,
Buffalo NY 14224

Copyright © 2023 by Greenhaven Publishing, LLC

First Edition

All rights reserved. No part of this book may be reproduced in any form without permission in writing from the publisher, except by a reviewer.

Articles in Greenhaven Publishing anthologies are often edited for length to meet page requirements. In addition, original titles of these works are changed to clearly present the main thesis and to explicitly indicate the author's opinion. Every effort is made to ensure that Greenhaven Publishing accurately reflects the original intent of the authors. Every effort has been made to trace the owners of the copyrighted material.

Cover image: Daniel Tadevosyan/Shutterstock.com

Library of Congress CataloginginPublication Data

Names: Karpan, Andrew, editor.
Title: Global trade and the supply chain / Andrew Karpan, book editor.
Description: First edition. | New York : Greenhaven Publishing, 2023. | Series: Opposing viewpoints | Includes bibliographical references. | Audience: Ages 15+. | Audience: Grades 10-12. | Summary: "Anthology of essays accompanied by original introductory material exploring the issue of global trade"-- Provided by publisher.
Identifiers: LCCN 2022021748 | ISBN 9781534509146 (library binding) | ISBN 9781534509139 (paperback)
Subjects: LCSH: International trade--Juvenile literature. | Business logistics--Juvenile literature.
Classification: LCC HF1379 .G58625 2023 | DDC 382--dc23/eng/20220504
LC record available at https://lccn.loc.gov/2022021748

Manufactured in the United States of America

Website: http://greenhavenpublishing.com

Contents

The Importance of Opposing Viewpoints   11
Introduction   14

Chapter 1: What Do Today's Supply Chains Look Like?

Chapter Preface   17

1. How COVID-19 Is Reshaping Supply Chains   19
   Knut Alicke, Ed Barriball, and Vera Trautwein

2. The Pandemic Revealed the Limitations of the Supply Chain System   26
   Sarah Schiffling and Nikolaos Valantasis Kanellos

3. The Economy Is Not a Linear Chain, but a Vast Dynamic Latticework   31
   Dan Sanchez

4. The War in Ukraine Could Drastically Reshape Global Supply Chains   35
   Tinglong Dai

Periodical and Internet Sources Bibliography   40

Chapter 2: How Have Supply Chains Evolved?

Chapter Preface   43

1. Supply Chains Are in Crisis, but Logistics Bosses Are Doing Better Than Ever   44
   Dave Braneck

2. The Pandemic Revealed Supply Chain Failures   53
   Chloé Farand

3. Why Don't Supply Chain Problems Occur More Often?   59
   Walter Block

4. Globalization Is Undergoing a Course Correction   63
   Rohinton Medhora

Periodical and Internet Sources Bibliography   68

Chapter 3: Can Trade Policy Be Used Effectively?

Chapter Preface   71

1. What's So Free About Trade?   72
   Brad McDonald

2. Tariffs Have Negative Effects on U.S. Employment   78
   The Economist

3. Alliances Bring Competitive Advantages and Also Risks   86
   Kathleen J. McInnis

4. Trade Reform Leads to Economic Growth   109
   Brian C. Albrecht

5. Multinationals Continue to Avoid Paying Hundreds of Billions of Dollars in Tax   115
   Miroslav Palanský

Periodical and Internet Sources Bibliography   120

Chapter 4: Is Globalization a Force for Good?

Chapter Preface   123

1. The Long Story of Trade Liberalization   124
   Raymon Huston and R. Adam Dastrup

2. Facing Our Global Environmental Challenges Requires Efficient International Cooperation   134
   Erik Lundberg

3. Globalization May Be Better for the Environment   139
   Sylvanus Kwaku Afesorgbor and Binyam Afewerk Demena

4. Does Globalization Breed Inequality?   145
   William Hauk

5. Wealth Inequality Is Everyone's Problem   149
   Market Business News

6. Global Trade Is the Way to Global Peace and Prosperity   155
   Marco den Ouden

Periodical and Internet Sources Bibliography   160

For Further Discussion	**162**
Organizations to Contact	**164**
Bibliography of Books	**169**
Index	**171**

The Importance of Opposing Viewpoints

Perhaps every generation experiences a period in time in which the populace seems especially polarized, starkly divided on the important issues of the day and gravitating toward the far ends of the political spectrum and away from a consensus-facilitating middle ground. The world that today's students are growing up in and that they will soon enter into as active and engaged citizens is deeply fragmented in just this way. Issues relating to terrorism, immigration, women's rights, minority rights, race relations, health care, taxation, wealth and poverty, the environment, policing, military intervention, the proper role of government—in some ways, perennial issues that are freshly and uniquely urgent and vital with each new generation—are currently roiling the world.

If we are to foster a knowledgeable, responsible, active, and engaged citizenry among today's youth, we must provide them with the intellectual, interpretive, and critical-thinking tools and experience necessary to make sense of the world around them and of the all-important debates and arguments that inform it. After all, the outcome of these debates will in large measure determine the future course, prospects, and outcomes of the world and its peoples, particularly its youth. If they are to become successful members of society and productive and informed citizens, students need to learn how to evaluate the strengths and weaknesses of someone else's arguments, how to sift fact from opinion and fallacy, and how to test the relative merits and validity of their own opinions against the known facts and the best possible available information. The landmark series Opposing Viewpoints has been providing students with just such critical-thinking skills and exposure to the debates surrounding society's most urgent contemporary issues for many years, and it continues to serve this essential role with undiminished commitment, care, and rigor.

The key to the series's success in achieving its goal of sharpening students' critical-thinking and analytic skills resides in its title—

Opposing Viewpoints. In every intriguing, compelling, and engaging volume of this series, readers are presented with the widest possible spectrum of distinct viewpoints, expert opinions, and informed argumentation and commentary, supplied by some of today's leading academics, thinkers, analysts, politicians, policy makers, economists, activists, change agents, and advocates. Every opinion and argument anthologized here is presented objectively and accorded respect. There is no editorializing in any introductory text or in the arrangement and order of the pieces. No piece is included as a "straw man," an easy ideological target for cheap point-scoring. As wide and inclusive a range of viewpoints as possible is offered, with no privileging of one particular political ideology or cultural perspective over another. It is left to each individual reader to evaluate the relative merits of each argument—as he or she sees it, and with the use of ever-growing critical-thinking skills—and grapple with his or her own assumptions, beliefs, and perspectives to determine how convincing or successful any given argument is and how the reader's own stance on the issue may be modified or altered in response to it.

This process is facilitated and supported by volume, chapter, and selection introductions that provide readers with the essential context they need to begin engaging with the spotlighted issues, with the debates surrounding them, and with their own perhaps shifting or nascent opinions on them. In addition, guided reading and discussion questions encourage readers to determine the authors' point of view and purpose, interrogate and analyze the various arguments and their rhetoric and structure, evaluate the arguments' strengths and weaknesses, test their claims against available facts and evidence, judge the validity of the reasoning, and bring into clearer, sharper focus the reader's own beliefs and conclusions and how they may differ from or align with those in the collection or those of their classmates.

Research has shown that reading comprehension skills improve dramatically when students are provided with compelling, intriguing, and relevant "discussable" texts. The subject matter of these collections could not be more compelling, intriguing, or urgently relevant to today's students and the world they are poised to inherit. The anthologized articles and the reading and discussion questions that are included with them also provide the basis for stimulating, lively, and passionate classroom debates. Students who are compelled to anticipate objections to their own argument and identify the flaws in those of an opponent read more carefully, think more critically, and steep themselves in relevant context, facts, and information more thoroughly. In short, using discussable text of the kind provided by every single volume in the Opposing Viewpoints series encourages close reading, facilitates reading comprehension, fosters research, strengthens critical thinking, and greatly enlivens and energizes classroom discussion and participation. The entire learning process is deepened, extended, and strengthened.

For all of these reasons, Opposing Viewpoints continues to be exactly the right resource at exactly the right time—when we most need to provide readers with the critical-thinking tools and skills that will not only serve them well in school but also in their careers and their daily lives as decision-making family members, community members, and citizens. This series encourages respectful engagement with and analysis of opposing viewpoints and fosters a resulting increase in the strength and rigor of one's own opinions and stances. As such, it helps make readers "future ready," and that readiness will pay rich dividends for the readers themselves, for the citizenry, for our society, and for the world at large.

Introduction

> "Within human economies, motives are assumed to be complex"
>
> —London School of Economics professor David Graeber, 2014.

Few inventions feel quite as instinctive as the supply chain. For economists, the story of civilization is the story of trade, and its most studied locations are trade's chainlinks of supply and demand. It was trade that created money, and it was trade that created debt, and it was trade that was behind every conflict and that motivated every great change in political fortune that had moved history along.

It is for this reason, perhaps, that supply chains around the world are so regularly and systematically studied. Whenever any event persists, the concern turns eventually to how it will impact the movement of products from border to border, how much products will cost consumers. It is the war on the other side of the world that has caused the increase in gas prices, or it is the hurricane in Florida that will change the price of oranges. Many of the viewpoints in this resource take a look at one event in particular: the outbreak of COVID-19 in 2020, an event that uniformly affected us all. The pandemic caused borders to shut down indefinitely and the economic world to nervously hold its breath as various methodologies were tested out to contain the novel illness. This was unlike anything that happened in a little over a century; the last notable pandemic had struck in 1918, in a world that was still largely connected by horseback.

Much of the supply chain as we know it today traced its origins to the 1970s and 1980s, the result of a storm of technological advancements taking place at a time when the world was seemingly in the middle of indefinite peace. The internet was the inadvertent creation of a packet-switching program at the U.S. Department of Defense for a future war. Before then, there was the personal computer, a glowing fusion of microchips and plastic boxes that could be manufactured anywhere. The biggest marketplace, however, was in the software industry. It was around this era that a change in U.S. labor regulation suddenly allowed trucking companies to reclassify their employees in order to run longer shifts, moving supply in greater volume.

During this time, incidentally, the environmental movement took notice of negative byproducts of an industrialized world. Factories had relocated to cheaper parts of the world, and the goods they manufactured had to be transported by shipping vessels. Manufacturing now left an ecological footprint that revealed the damage involved in producing and delivering goods to consumers worldwide.

The political response to the establishment of global geopolitics remains ongoing. The populist political campaigns of 2016, which resulted in the United Kingdom's departure from the European Union, as well as the election of Donald Trump to the U.S. presidency, were read as rejections of the implications of globalization, which had first transformed the rest of the world before returning home to transform social relations. Neither movement, however, proved capable of fundamentally turning those revolutions around and instead turned to modulating trade policy.

Opposing Viewpoints: Global Trade and the Supply Chain is a survey of that debate. In chapters titled "What Do Today's Supply Chains Look Like?," How Have Supply Chains Evolved?," "Can Trade Policy Be Used Effectively?," and "Is Globalization a Force for Good?," viewpoint authors explore the complex network of interconnecting factors that affect so many aspects of our lives.

CHAPTER 1

What Do Today's Supply Chains Look Like?

Chapter Preface

When borders shuttered simultaneously around the world in an effort to contain the spread of the COVID-19 virus, it wasn't only tourists who were forced to cancel their travel plans. Workers, from seasonal employees to conference-trotting executives, were being held from their labor, lingering on the sidelines of the economy, on indefinite pause. As stores closed, factories pulled production to deal with thinner demand, resulting in mass layoffs. Shippers, in turn, kept much of the world's massive supply of shipping containers docked at home, anticipating a decrease in product to ship out.

The immediate impact of these sudden contractions was in the numbers, which were geographically unrelenting. Nowhere in the world, it seemed, was there an economic ecosystem that wasn't in some way suddenly tilting downward. What the moment revealed, however, was that the current system of logistics, so apt at wiggling around in real time to changing needs and wants, was equally unable to successfully predict what people wanted or needed. There were certainly surges in demand—for personal protective equipment, for respirators, for doctors who were now needed to treat millions of newly sick people. Instead of waiting around for stores to reopen safely, consumers everywhere conducted their shopping online, quickly emptying undersupplied warehouses around the world. Entire professions that were once based on constant movement suddenly were being moved to digital spaces.

But instead of accommodating these new surges in demand, shipping crates were sitting in ports unused. Scammers were making promises they could never fill. There was a seemingly endless amount of money waiting to be spent on supplies like medical-grade masks, for instance, but the largest medical supply companies in the world discovered they were unable to meet these immediate needs at any price. Laid-off workers were now suddenly needed, and goods were gathering in piles around the world until they could be found.

These nervous bumps show something of how today's supply chains operate. They are machines of enormous planning that are liable to collapse at the touch of a crisis and are immobile amid a fog of unpredictability. Many of the viewpoints in the following chapter explore these crises and search through their reporting to find a message about how our supply chain should respond to future shocks. Others look deeper into the past and farther into the future to find other issues.

VIEWPOINT 1

> *"Companies were much more likely than expected to increase inventories, and much less likely either to diversify supply bases … or to implement nearshoring or regionalization strategies."*

How COVID-19 Is Reshaping Supply Chains

Knut Alicke, Ed Barriball, and Vera Trautwein

In the following viewpoint, Knut Alicke, Ed Barriball, and Vera Trautwein examine supply chain issues caused by the COVID-19 pandemic. The authors focus on four major takeaways: inventory building, risk management, planning, and digitization. They conclude that supply chains remain at risk even while leaders are abandoning the progress they achieved during the most urgent period of the pandemic. Knut Alicke is a partner in the Stuttgart office of McKinsey & Company. Ed Barriball is a partner in McKinsey's Washington, D.C., office. Vera Trautwein is an expert in McKinsey's Zurich office.

As you read, consider the following questions:

1. When did McKinsey conduct its two surveys studying pandemic-related supply chain disruptions?

"How COVID-19 Is Reshaping Supply Chains," by Knut Alicke, Ed Barriball, and Vera Trautwein, McKinsey & Company, November 23, 2021. This article was originally published by McKinsey & Company, www.mckinsey.com . Copyright ©2022 All rights reserved. Reprinted by permission.

2. How did the pandemic prioritize risk for most companies?
3. How has supply chain digitization changed during the pandemic?

In May 2020, much of the world was still in the grip of the first wave of the COVID-19 pandemic. Lockdowns, shelter-in-place orders, and travel restrictions were disrupting activity in every part of the economy. Demand evaporated in some categories and skyrocketed in others. As they struggled to keep their businesses running, companies were planning significant strategic changes to the configuration and operation of their supply chains. When we surveyed senior supply-chain executives from across industries and geographies, 93 percent of respondents told us that they intended to make their supply chains far more flexible, agile, and resilient.

Twelve months later, in the second quarter of 2021, we repeated our survey with a similarly diverse group of supply-chain leaders. This time, we asked respondents to describe the steps they had taken to shore up their supply chains over the past year, how those changes compared with the plans they drew up earlier in the crisis, and how they expect their supply chains to further evolve in the coming months and years.

It's Quicker to Build Inventories than Factories

In our 2020 survey, just over three-quarters of respondents told us they planned to improve resilience through physical changes to their supply-chain footprints. By this year, an overwhelming majority (92 percent) said that they had done so.

But our survey revealed significant shifts in footprint strategy. Last year, most companies planned to pull multiple levers in their efforts to improve supply-chain resilience, combining increases in the inventory of critical products, components, and materials with efforts to diversify supply bases while localizing or regionalizing supply and production networks. In practice, companies were much more likely than expected to increase inventories, and much less likely either to diversify supply bases (with raw-material supply being a notable exception) or to implement nearshoring or regionalization strategies

Different industries have responded to the resilience challenge in markedly different ways. Healthcare players stand out as resilience leaders. They applied the broadest range of measures, with 60 percent of healthcare respondents saying they had regionalized their supply chains and 33 percent having moved production closer to end markets. By contrast, only 22 percent of automotive, aerospace, and defense players had regionalized production, even though more than three-quarters of them prioritized this approach in their answers to the 2020 survey. Chemicals and commodity players made the smallest overall changes to their supply-chain footprints during the past year.

Some of these differences among sectors can be attributed to the structural characteristics of the industries involved: for example, chemicals and metals are asset-intensive sectors with large, expensive production sites. Investments in new capacity can take years to complete. Other respondents told us that they had struggled to find suitable suppliers to support their localization or near-shoring plans.

Despite these challenges, regionalization remains a priority for most companies. Almost 90 percent of respondents told us that they expect to pursue some degree of regionalization during the next three years, and 100 percent of respondents from both the healthcare and the engineering, construction, and infrastructure sectors said the approach was relevant to their sector.

Risk Management: More Breadth, Not Enough Depth

The pandemic pushed risk to the top of virtually every corporate agenda. For the first time, most respondents (95 percent) say they have formal supply-chain risk-management processes. A further 59 percent of companies say they have adopted new supply-chain risk management-practices over the past 12 months. A small minority (4 percent) set up a new risk-management function from scratch, but most respondents say they have strengthened existing capabilities.

The actions taken by companies varied according to the precrisis maturity of their supply-chain risk-management capabilities. Companies with little or no risk-management experience tended to invest in new software tools, while higher-maturity organizations mainly focused on the implementation of new practices.

The proactive monitoring of supplier risks was the primary focus of these efforts, yet significant blind spots remain in most companies' supply-chain risk-management setups. Just under half of the companies in our survey say they understand the location of their tier-one suppliers and the key risks those suppliers face. But only 2 percent can make the same claim about suppliers in the third tier and beyond. That matters because many of today's most pressing supply shortages, such as semiconductors, happen in these deeper supply-chain tiers.

Supply-Chain Planning: A Test for Technology and Organization

The transition to remote working was one of the most immediate and pronounced effects of pandemic-era restrictions on mobility and access to workplaces. Broadly, respondents to our survey believe they managed that transition well, with 58 percent reporting good supply-chain-planning performance over the past year. The remaining 42 percent of respondents told us that remote working had led to delays in supply-chain decision making.

The success of an organization's planning was strongly linked to its use of modern digital tools, especially advanced analytics. Compared with organizations that reported problems, successful companies were 2.5 times more likely to report they had preexisting advanced-analytics capabilities. Of the companies that had difficulties managing their supply chains during the crisis, 71 percent say they are ramping up their use of advanced analytics.

The benefits of advanced analytics in supply-chain management are now being recognized across industries. With the sole exception of the healthcare sector, more than 50 percent of respondents in every industry say they have implemented additional analytics approaches during the past 12 months. The biggest shifts occurred in industries that were the lowest users of these approaches before the pandemic. In commodities, for example, 75 percent of companies are currently increasing their use, with the remaining 25 percent saying they plan to do so in the future. The only sector in which the race to adopt advanced analytics techniques shows signs of slowing down is in advanced electronics and high tech, where their adoption is already very high.

Digitization Surges but Could Tail Off

With so much interest in advanced analytics, it comes as little surprise that the crisis has been a catalyst for further digitization of end-to-end supply-chain processes. An overwhelming majority of survey respondents say they have invested in digital supply-chain technologies during the past year, with most investing more than they originally planned. While automotive and commodity players were reluctant to commit to additional investments amid the uncertainty of early 2020, for example, 100 percent of the respondents in those sectors eventually did so. Almost every company also plans for further digital investment in the future. Construction is the only sector in which respondents say they are less likely to invest in digital supply chain technologies in the coming years.

Today's ongoing and planned digitization efforts are most likely to focus on visibility, as companies strive for a better picture of their supply chains' real-time performance. For example, since May 2020, 30 percent of respondents had implemented new digital performance-management systems—an important enabler of supply-chain visibility. Improved planning tools, either for specific aspects of the supply chain (such as logistics management) or broader end-to-end planning systems, come a close second among the companies in our survey, with more than three-quarters saying they were a priority. Just under half of all respondents also say they are looking at network-modeling tools to help them improve supply-chain design in the longer term. Nevertheless, despite the prevalence and impact of supply-chain shocks over the past two years, only 39 percent of companies are investing in tools to monitor risks and disruptions.

Talent remains a major barrier to accelerated digitization, however, and the skills gap is widening. In our 2020 survey, only 10 percent of companies said they had sufficient in-house digital talent. And by this year, that figure had dropped dramatically, to only 1 percent. Respondents report a range of ongoing actions to address the digital-skills gap, including reskilling (55 percent) or redeploying (30 percent) existing staff, hiring new talent from the labor market (52 percent), and taking on specialist contract staff for specific projects (21 percent).

Next Steps: Supply Chains at an Inflection Point

The COVID-19 crisis put supply chains into the spotlight. Over the past year, supply-chain leaders have taken decisive action in response to the challenges of the pandemic: adapting effectively to new ways of working, boosting inventories, and ramping their digital and risk-management capabilities. Yet despite that progress, other recent events have shown that supply chains remain vulnerable to shocks and disruptions, with many sectors currently wrestling to overcome supply-side shortages and logistics-capacity constraints. Most worryingly, these new problems are emerging just as senior leaders are turning their attention away from supply-chain issues. In many sectors, there are signs that the rate of investment in digital supply-chain technologies is slowing down. Talent gaps are wider than ever, end-to-end transparency remains elusive, and progress toward more localized, flexible supply-chain structures has been slower than anticipated.

The coming months could turn out to be critical for supply-chain leaders. Some companies will build upon the momentum they gained during the pandemic, with decisive action to adapt their supply-chain footprint, modernize their technologies, and build their capabilities. Others may slip back, reverting to old ways of working that leave them struggling to compete with their more agile competitors on cost or service, and still vulnerable to shocks and disruptions.

VIEWPOINT

| *"Ultimately, supply chains are driven by people."*

The Pandemic Revealed the Limitations of the Supply Chain System

Sarah Schiffling and Nikolaos Valantasis Kanellos

In the following viewpoint, writers Sarah Schiffling and Nikolaos Valantasis Kanellos use the recent experience of the COVID-19 pandemic to explore the larger elasticity of supply chain problems. Supply shortages are what make the headlines and evoke the empty shelves of supermarkets. This becomes a problem because the modern economy relies on the constant streams of capital that these day-to-day transactions represent. But in a globally connected world, behind every supply shortage is a supply surplus somewhere else. Sarah Schiffling teaches supply chain management at Liverpool John Moores University. Nikolaos Valantasis Kanellos teaches logistics at Technological University Dublin.

As you read, consider the following questions:

1. Technological changes have transformed manufacturing, but why hasn't this had a major import on modern supply chains?

"Supply Chains in 2022: Shortages Will Continue, but for Some Sellers the Problem Will Be Too Much Stock," by Sarah Schiffling and Nikolaos Valantasis Kanellos, The Conversation, January 7, 2022. https://theconversation.com/supply-chains-in-2022-shortages-will-continue-but-for-some-sellers-the-problem-will-be-too-much-stock-174085. Licensed under CC BY-4.0 International.

2. What kind of problems are caused by oversupply?
3. What caused supply shortages at the start of the COVID-19 pandemic?

Everything was about shortages in 2021. COVID vaccine shortages at the start of the year were replaced by fears that we would struggle to buy turkeys, toys or electronic gizmos to put under the Christmas tree. For most of the year, supermarket shelves, car showrooms and even petrol stations were emptier than usual. Some shortages were resolved quickly, others linger. So are we facing another year of shortages or will the supply chain crisis abate in 2022?

It's worth reflecting that the shortages have happened for many reasons. During the early 2020 lockdowns, a sudden run on essentials such as toilet paper and pasta left shelves around the world bare. Singapore ran out of eggs as consumers hoarded them, for example. Retailers ordered more eggs, desperate to satisfy demand. But once the demand had been satisfied, there was suddenly an oversupply. In June of that year, distributors threw away 250,000 eggs.

This is what happens when demand temporarily changes. The effect magnifies with each tier of the supply chain as every supplier adds an extra buffer to their order to be on the safe side. Minute changes in customer demand can therefore result in huge extra demand for raw materials. This is called the bullwhip effect. As with a whip, a small flick of the wrist can lead to a big crack at the other end.

The bullwhip effect can be from demand suddenly falling as well as rising, and during the pandemic these forces have sometimes combined. For instance, a combination of the crash in demand for new cars and higher demand for devices like laptops and games consoles for lockdown entertainment contributed to the semiconductor-chip shortage.

With modern cars sometimes containing 3,000 chips, car makers are major customers for chips. But as car sales plummeted in 2020, supplies of chips were redirected to manufacturers of smaller electronic goods. When demand for cars picked up again a few months later, there were not enough chips to go around. Carmakers were forced to stop production lines and couldn't make enough cars to satisfy demand. They also started hoarding chips, making the shortages worse.

Shipping Shenanigans

Other imbalances in today's supply chains are larger than competing companies or industries. Shipping containers move some 1.9 billion tonnes per year by sea alone, including virtually all imported fruits, gadgets and appliances. Normally containers are continually loaded, shipped, unloaded and loaded again, but severe trade disruptions resulting from lockdowns and border closures broke that cycle.

Containers were left in wrong locations as trade shifted, shipping capacity was reduced and vessels couldn't land where and when they intended. Coupled with congested ports and problems with timely unloading and onward transportation, a typical container now spends 20% longer in transit than before the pandemic.

Shipping rates have soared in this environment. Prices on major east-west trade routes have increased by 80% year on year, which is bad news for economic recovery. Even a 10% increase in container freight rates can reduce industrial production by around 1%.

The Human Factor

Technological advancement may have reshaped manufacturing, but production and delivery still rely heavily on people. Waves of layoffs in production due to lockdowns resulted in labour shortages when demand picked up. To give one example, Vietnam saw a mass exodus of workers from industrial hubs to rural areas, which could not easily be reversed.

Worker shortages were particularly evident with lorry drivers in the UK and other countries. The sector already struggled to recruit and retain drivers because of pressures of rising demand, an ageing workforce and worsening working conditions. Meanwhile, Brexit has made it harder for migrant drivers to work in the UK.

There were at least early signs of the driver problems easing in the run-up to Christmas as more recruits came through the system, which will have been one reason why goods shortages were not as bad as they might have been. Equally, however, we shouldn't expect a swift end to the supply chain crisis in 2022.

The omicron variant is leading to more staff shortages as people take time off sick and suppliers navigate new restrictions. China's zero-COVID strategy is likely to continue to disrupt both production and transportation of goods, possibly for the entire year.

Yet we might also see problems in the opposite direction, via another crack of the bullwhip. Back-orders in many sectors will have been filled, but consumer demand may well be cooling now that furloughs have ended and interest rates are beginning to rise. So some companies might find they end up with an over-supply of goods.

To avoid this, they will have to level their production rates with demand. Yet demand may still be difficult to forecast – and not only because of omicron and China. A new variant of concern leading to a new wave of lockdowns could easily result in people once again spending money on things rather than holidays and nights out. Supply chains with good visibility of actual demand and clear communication across supply chain tiers will be at a considerable advantage. In sum, it is likely that different industries will experience both shortages and over-supply problems throughout 2022.

A longer-term issue is to what extent supply chains change. The pandemic raised new doubts about outsourcing production to far-away countries with lower labour costs. Equally, problems were aggravated by strategies to maximise supply-chain efficiency such as just-in-time manufacturing, where companies keep inventories to a bare minimum to reduce costs.

A major theme of 2021 was how to make supply chains more resilient. But building additional capacity, holding inventory and safeguarding against disruptions is not cheap. As shipping logjams ease and recruitment rises, the talk of reform could peter out. Some companies will probably continue to improve their just-in-time with a sprinkle of just-in-case. Others will bring production of some products closer to home markets while also keeping offshore production facilities to serve local markets. It also remains to be seen to what extent COVID reverses globalisation.

Ultimately, supply chains are driven by people, and 2021 showed the limitations of the system. As companies and consumers adapt, current knots will untangle somewhat. But as the pandemic wears on and the realities of keeping businesses profitable come back to the fore, you probably shouldn't expect a resolution in 2022.

Viewpoint 3

> "The fatal conceit of central planners is manifest in the very term 'global supply chain.'"

The Economy Is Not a Linear Chain, but a Vast Dynamic Latticework

Dan Sanchez

In the following viewpoint Dan Sanchez argues that attempts by central governments to influence the supply chain by intervening create more harm than good. This has been evidenced by government shutdowns during the COVID-19 pandemic. The author contends that goods are produced from a vast network that is self-corrected by the actions of the market. Dan Sanchez is the Director of Content at the Foundation for Economic Education (FEE) and the editor-in chief of FEE.org.

As you read, consider the following questions:

1. Why does a lockdown in China affect people in the United States?
2. What purpose does the author's example of the production of a pencil serve?
3. What does the author consider to be tyranny?

"The Shanghai Lockdown and the "Supply Chain" Fallacy," by Dan Sanchez, Foundation for Economic Education, April 8, 2022, https://fee.org/articles/the-shanghai-lockdown-and-the-supply-chain-fallacy/. Licensed under CC BY-4.0 International.

The virus that locked down the world has returned to China in full force. And I don't mean the Wuhan coronavirus.

Nearly every world government emulated China's authoritarian response to Covid-19. That is what sent civilization spiraling into crisis, not the coronavirus itself. The mind virus of central planning, as applied to epidemic diseases, spread from the Chinese Communist Party to the halls of power throughout the "free world." That ideological pandemic is a far more dire threat to humanity than any superbug.

Now China's fever for authoritarian "public health" policy has spiked again. As The Wall Street Journal reported yesterday, "Stringent government measures to contain the country's Covid-19 outbreak, the worst in more than two years, are locking down tens of millions of people, mostly in and around the industrial heartland of Shanghai."

This has been a nightmare for those tens of millions directly impacted. And the economic havoc will not be quarantined in China. It will reach us all.

"Manufacturers are struggling to keep some of their China operations going," according to the Journal, as the expanded lockdowns "choke off supplies and clog up truck routes and ports, heaping more pressure on the stretched global supply chain."

Tim Huxley, chairman of a Hong Kong container ship company, warned Journal readers that the supply bottleneck will have major consequences for western consumers. "It's anything from electronic goods, domestic goods, furniture—you name a household brand or chain store in the U.S. or Europe and you can bet they will have something stuck in a factory on a truck coming out of Shanghai."

This means even higher prices, lower availability, and less selection—in other words, a reduced quality of life—for us all.

Again, it will not be the coronavirus making us poorer, but the fallacy, embraced by officials from Beijing to DC, that central planners can manage society-wide problems, like "healing" a global pandemic or "fixing" a global supply chain.

WHAT IS SUSTAINABILITY?

The most often quoted definition comes from the UN World Commission on Environment and Development: "sustainable development is development that meets the needs of the present without compromising the ability of future generations to meet their own needs."

In the charter for the UCLA Sustainability Committee, sustainability is defined as: "the integration of environmental health, social equity and economic vitality in order to create thriving, healthy, diverse and resilient communities for this generation and generations to come. The practice of sustainability recognizes how these issues are interconnected and requires a systems approach and an acknowledgement of complexity."

Sustainable practices support ecological, human, and economic health and vitality. Sustainability presumes that resources are finite, and should be used conservatively and wisely with a view to long-term priorities and consequences of the ways in which resources are used. In simplest terms, sustainability is about our children and our grandchildren, and the world we will leave them.

"What Is Sustainability?" by the Sustainability Committee at the University of California, Los Angeles.

As the great economists Ludwig von Mises and F.A. Hayek explained, societies and economies are inconceivably complex, and it is literally impossible for anyone to centrally plan something so far beyond their comprehension. To think otherwise is, as Hayek called it, a "fatal conceit."

The fatal conceit of central planners is manifest in the very term "global supply chain." The metaphor of a "chain" portrays the economy as something static and linear: something simple enough for a single mind to "fix."

But, as Leonard Read vividly showed in his classic essay "I, Pencil," even a seemingly simple good like a pencil is not the product of a single supply chain. Every good in the economy is descended from a vast "family tree" of innumerable factors of production. And all the family trees of all goods are intricately interconnected, making the economy, not a "chain," but as economist Murray Rothbard depicted it, "a highly complex, interacting latticework of exchanges."

This vast, dynamic latticework is self-healing and self-fixing: through the actions and interactions of its constituent individuals. Blundering, arrogant central planners only get in the way and make things worse.

That has been the lesson of free-market economists and social theorists going back to Adam Smith. The western world partly embraced that lesson, and it flourished as a result, becoming a beacon to the world. Starting in the 1970s, even Communist China emulated its example, opening up its markets. This was a humanitarian miracle for the Chinese people and a boon for us all. If not for Chinese manufacturing being integrated into the global division of labor, it is hard to imagine the west having the modern high-tech living standards and super-comfortable working conditions we enjoy (however precariously) today.

Whereas once China liberalized in emulation of the west, now the leaders of the "free world" are emulating (and, in the case of Canada's prime minister, openly admiring) the authoritarianism of the CCP. As crises continue to mount, it is clear that this turn toward tyranny is putting our future at risk.

If we don't want the prosperity and material security we have built up over generations to vanish, we must rediscover the ideas and principles that created it in the first place.

VIEWPOINT 4

> *"While the direct effects of the war on supply chains are relatively limited, the impact on the global movement of goods and services has been significant."*

The War in Ukraine Could Drastically Reshape Global Supply Chains

Tinglong Dai

In the following viewpoint Tinglong Dai argues that Russia's 2022 attack on Ukraine could have lasting effects on the global supply chain and economy, even more so than the COVID-19 pandemic. The author predicts that a new supply chain division will emerge, with the West on one side and Russia and its allies on the other. Tinglong Dai is Professor of Operations Management and Business Analytics at the John Hopkins Carey Business School.

As you read, consider the following questions:

1. What event was considered the "end of history"?
2. What was one immediate effect of the Russian invasion felt by Americans?
3. What does McDonald's have to do with the supply chain?

"Ukraine War and Anti-Russia Sanctions on Top of COVID-19 Mean Even Worse Trouble Lies Ahead for Global Supply Chains," by Tinglong Dai, The Conversation, March 11, 2022, https://theconversation.com/ukraine-war-and-anti-russia-sanctions-on-top-of-covid-19-mean-even-worse-trouble-lies-ahead-for-global-supply-chains-178486. Licensed under CC BY-ND 4.0.

Francis Fukuyama, the American political scientist who once described the collapse of the Soviet Union as the "end of history," suggested that Russia's invasion of Ukraine might be called "the end of the end of history." He meant that Vladimir Putin's aggression signals a rollback of the ideals of a free Europe that emerged after 1991. Some observers suggest it may kick off a new Cold War, with an Iron Curtain separating the West from Russia.

As an expert in global supply chains, I think the war portends the end of something else: global supply chains that Western companies built after the Berlin Wall fell over three decades ago.

Supply chains—often vast networks of resources, money, information and people that companies rely on to get goods or services to consumers—were already in disarray because of the COVID-19 pandemic, resulting in massive shortages, disruptions and price inflation. The war and resulting sanctions against Russia have immediately put further strains on them, prompting skyrocketing energy prices and even fears of famine.

But beyond these short-term effects, I believe the war in Ukraine could drastically reshape global supply chains in a way the pandemic never did.

Immediate Effects: Fuel and Famine

Russia accounts for less than 2% of global gross domestic product, while Ukraine accounts for only 0.14%. As a result, they have little direct impact on global supply chains—except in a few very important areas.

Let's start with the most obvious one: energy. Russia supplies nearly 40% of Europe's natural gas supply and 65% of Germany's. It is the third-largest oil exporter in the world, accounting for 7% of all crude oil and petroleum product imports into the United States. After the Biden administration signaled it would stop importing Russian oil, the price of crude topped US$130 per barrel for the first time in 13 years, and consumers in some parts of the U.S. have seen average gasoline prices rise above $5 per gallon.

Less obviously, Russia and Ukraine account for nearly one-third of all global wheat exports. Several countries, including Kazakhstan and Tanzania, import more than 90% of their wheat from Russia. The war has the potential to disrupt the still-recovering global food supply chain and endanger the livelihoods of millions of people.

Even less obviously, Ukraine produces 90% of the semiconductor-grade neon used in the United States. Russia, on the other hand, provides the United States more than a third of its palladium, a rare metal also required to make semiconductors. Although companies have enough inventory to fulfill immediate needs and may find alternative suppliers, some disruptions are inevitable. And this comes at a time when the world is still suffering from a severe chip shortage, which has slowed auto production and sent new and used car prices soaring.

It is also worth noting that Russia is a dominant exporter of titanium and titanium forgings, which are popular in the aerospace industry because of their light weight. This war will further stress the aerospace supply chain.

Snarling Trade

While the direct effects of the war on supply chains are relatively limited, the impact on the global movement of goods and services has been significant—I believe even greater than from COVID-19.

After 36 countries, including EU members, the U.S. and Canada, closed their airspace to Russian aircraft, Russia retaliated with the same restrictions. As a result, goods transported by air freight from China to Europe or the Eastern U.S. may need to be rerouted or use slower or more expensive modes of transportation. The China-Europe rail freight route that goes through Russia, which was experiencing a boom in 2021 because of congestion in major ports, now faces mounting cancellations from European clients.

The war has also had a devastating impact on global trade movements, with hundreds of tankers and bulk carriers stranded at ports as a result of sanctions imposed on Russian-connected ships. It has also resulted in severe travel and transport restrictions imposed on Russia and Belarus in an unprecedentedly rapid and broad manner that has been coordinated among multiple nations.

In addition, the disruption of the route from China to Europe and the U.S. could do severe damage to China's "Belts and Roads" initiative. That's the ambitious trillion-dollar project aimed at reshaping global trade and affirming the dominance of a China-centric global supply chain, especially in Europe and Asia. Because both Russia and Ukraine are critical links in the initiative, it will almost certainly need to scale back in size and scope.

A Supply Chain Iron Curtain

The New York Times columnist Thomas Friedman, a true believer in globalization, in 1996 famously theorized that no two countries that both have a McDonald's would ever fight a war against each other. McDonald's has about 850 restaurants in Russia and 100 in Ukraine, all of which have now been temporarily closed.

His point was that countries with economies and middle classes big enough to support a McDonald's "don't like to fight wars; they like to wait in line for burgers." It was also based on the belief that rational economic calculations will always triumph over geopolitical conflicts—that is, leaders in such countries wouldn't let their differences get in the way of trade and making money.

And the supply chains that companies erected in the decades since then have crisscrossed the globe, ignoring old enemy lines for the sake of efficiency and higher profits.

Friedman now concedes Russia's action has shattered that theory. I agree, and in fact the world may now be on the cusp of a new type of supply chain Iron Curtain with Russia and its allies on one side and the West on the other. Companies will no longer be able to separate business from geopolitics.

And those allies include China, which remains pivotal to most Western companies' supply chains. Despite China's ambiguous stance on the invasion, the war will likely serve as a catalyst to reduce that dependence, at least for critical products such as materials used for semiconductor manufacturing, medical supplies and electric batteries.

Moreover, the growing emphasis of shareholders and regulators on environmental, social and governance issues means how a company does in each category can affect its daily operations and cost of capital. On the issue of Ukraine, the push to be more socially responsible is one reason companies have overcomplied with sanctions. It's also prompting them to proactively avoid geopolitical risks, which can involve retreating from an entire economy.

Russia's war against Ukraine is still ongoing, and there's no way to know for certain how long the sanctions will remain in place or whether companies that have chosen to leave Russia will return. But I believe one thing is certain: Global supply chains, like the rest of the world, will never be the same again as a result of this war.

Periodical and Internet Sources Bibliography

The following articles have been selected to supplement the diverse views presented in this chapter.

Rica Bhattacharyya and Shailesh Menon, "They have not returned," *Economic Times*, September 25, 2021. https://economictimes.indiatimes.com/news/economy/indicators/they-have-not-returned-how-covid-19-has-impacted-labour-migration-in-the-country/articleshow/86513113.cms.

Ben Casselman and Ana Swanson, "Supply Chain Hurdles Will Outlast Pandemic, White House Says," *New York Times*, April 14, 2022, https://www.nytimes.com/2022/04/14/business/economy/biden-supply-chain.html.

Amy Davidson Sorkin, "The Supply-Chain Mystery," *New Yorker,* September 26, 2021. https://www.newyorker.com/magazine/2021/10/04/the-supply-chain-mystery.

Dave Davies, "The global supply chain is amazingly efficient. So why did it break down?," NPR, January 5, 2022. https://www.npr.org/2022/01/05/1070514847/the-global-supply-chain-arriving-today-christopher-mims.

Michelle Fleury, "How will the US deal with a shortage of 80,000 truckers?," BBC, November 8 2021. https://www.bbc.com/news/business-59136957#:~:text=The%20American%20Trucking%20Associations%20(ATA,160%2C000%20over%20the%20next%20decade.

Peter S. Goodman, "A Normal Supply Chain? It's 'Unlikely' in 2022.," *New York Times*, February 1, 2022. https://www.nytimes.com/2022/02/01/business/supply-chain-disruption.html.

Eric Levitz, "6 Signs That the Supply-Chain Crisis Is (Slowly) Ending," *New York Magazine*, November 22, 2021. https://nymag.com/intelligencer/2021/11/6-signs-that-the-supply-chain-crisis-is-slowly-ending.html.

Sarah Nassauer, "Walmart Raises Forecast and Says Shelves Are Stocked for Holiday Shoppers," *Wall Street Journal*, November 16, 2021. https://www.wsj.com/articles/walmart-raises-forecast-and-says-shelves-are-stocked-for-holiday-shoppers-11637066985.

Costas Paris, "Ocean Shipping Rates Fall but Ports Are Still Jammed," *Wall Street Journal*, November 15, 2021. https://www.wsj.com/articles/ocean-shipping-rates-fall-but-ports-are-still-jammed-11636972201?mod=article_inline.

Alina Selyukh, "Warehouses are overwhelmed by America's shopping spree," NPR, November 15, 2021. https://www.npr.org/2021/11/15/1055796115/warehouses-are-overwhelmed-by-americas-shopping-spree.

Brooke Sutherland, "The U.S. Supply-Chain Crisis Is Already Easing," *Bloomberg*, November 18, 2021. https://www.bloomberg.com/opinion/articles/2021-11-18/the-u-s-supply-chain-crisis-is-already-easing?sref=ZtdQlmKR

Stella Yifan Xie, Jon Emont and Alistair MacDonald, "Supply-Chain Problems Show Signs of Easing," *Wall Street Journal*, November 21, 2021 . https://www.wsj.com/articles/supply-chain-problems-show-signs-of-easing-11637496002?mod=rsswn.

OPPOSING VIEWPOINTS® SERIES

CHAPTER 2

How Have Supply Chains Evolved?

Chapter Preface

In most stores in the Western world, the expectation is that you can find almost anything, almost any time of the year. And if you can't, you can order it online. A lot of economists see this as a modern creation—the result of a revolution in logistics that took place in the 1970s and 1980s. It was then that commercial shipping really took off, following labor and shipping deregulations that began in the 1970s. Soon enough, products that were once regularly made in American manufacturing centers were now being made, far more cheaply, in countries with different standards of living. In turn, products became cheaper, which only caused demand to accelerate as people realized they could afford more and became accustomed to that convenience.

It wasn't only shipping that changed things, however. While shipping boxes around the world may seem low-tech, the simultaneous revolution in computing had made it possible to move products in ways that were previously thought only theoretical but now were the basis for an entire industry. By 1989, approximately one-third of the entire software industry—$1.2 billion—was dedicated to powering software that manufacturers used to get goods around the world.

But this revolution in distribution did not occur equally. While food from all over the world filled shelves in grocery stores in the west, even the smallest contraction in the larger supply chain often meant starvation to those on its edges. Entire economies were also deliberately excluded from this marketplace. For example, the U.S. used its military and economic power to issue sanctions against Iran's leadership after students in Tehran held a number of American diplomats, among others, hostage in 1979. Such countries present a different way of looking at how the supply chain has impacted people around the world.

The following chapter looks to that recent history to present a picture of how changes in managing logistics have a lot to do with the world as we see it today. The viewpoint authors offer several different takes on how positive a change that development has been and how it should look in the future.

VIEWPOINT 1

> "While we finally have evidence of the widespread vulnerability of supply chains, seeing just what it takes to seriously hurt them is an unsavory taste of reality for workers."

Supply Chains Are in Crisis, but Logistics Bosses Are Doing Better Than Ever
Dave Braneck

In the following excerpted viewpoint, Dave Braneck argues that the seeds of modern capitalism were sown during the deregulation regimes of the 1970s and 1980s. Braneck is critical of these changes and argues that they have given workers less power in a global marketplace that he says has become a collective "race-to-the-bottom" in terms of wages and living conditions. He writes that these new problems are justified by those who advocated for them as needed to create a supply chain that was flexible enough meet the needs of a globalized world. Dave Braneck is a freelance writer based in Berlin.

As you read, consider the following questions:

1. Before the "logistics revolution" of the 1970s and 1980s, what was the employment status of most truck drivers in the United States?

"Supply Chains Are in Crisis, but Logistics Bosses Are Doing Better Than Ever," by Dave Braneck, Jacobin Magazine, December 15, 2021. Reprinted by permission.

2. What was considered the greatest asset of the new logistics infrastructure that was created by these changes to the labor market?
3. What is one term for parts of a supply chain that are "capable of pressuring, or even stopping, global capitalism," and how did they come to be?

[…]

A combination of issues has produced the most striking images of the crisis, from unloaded containers stacked perilously high at some of the world's largest ports, to hulking container ships floating idly as they wait to bring their cargo to shore. At the height of this global gridlock a record 111 containers were waiting off Los Angeles and neighboring Long Beach ports, smashing the pre-pandemic high of seventeen. Roughly 40 percent of US container traffic comes through these southern California ports.

Though most acute in California, there have also been massive delays in ports from Savannah, Georgia to Newark, New Jersey—and, indeed, in Britain, the Netherlands, and China, with roughly six hundred cargo ships globally left waiting to unload at one point last month. Clogged ports created bottlenecks so dire that Joe Biden was roused from his nap to decree the LA and Long Beach ports would shift to 24/7 operations to ease pressure. And while a global, static flotilla loaded with late deliveries is hard to ignore, it's only one factor in the crisis.

While in Europe consumer demand is yet to fully recover from the pandemic, it has exploded in the United States. This is partly due to the pandemic spurring rare, if inadequate, direct public support for consumers. US household income rose 10.5 percent in April 2020 amid mass joblessness and shutdowns, as beefed-up unemployment benefits kicked in, bringing many Americans more cash than they normally got at work. Similarly, consumer spending rose 4.2 percent on the back of the third round of stimulus investment this spring.

Most Americans spent more in 2021 than last year, while consumption of many goods has eclipsed 2019's pre-pandemic levels. Global production has struggled to meet this skyrocketing demand, with various hiccups further slowing trade and heaping pressure on links in the supply chain. Thanks to high demand and the abundance of backed up ports, there's even a shortage of shipping containers.

Given how much the pandemic has impacted nearly every facet of life all over the world, it's a wonder that the Global North has only just begun to feel the supply chain crunch in earnest. The effects of the pandemic have, doubtless, been strongly differentiated across the planet. But just as COVID-19 initially spread along globalized routes of production and trade, the virus continues to impact global production. As the Delta variant spread to Asia this Spring, some of the busiest ports in the world were shuttered due to COVID outbreaks. Similar slowdowns have recently hit factories in China and Vietnam, key global industrial producers.

Knock-on effects of pandemic outbreaks straining extraction and production, along with sustained demand, have fostered further bottlenecks in supply chains. Prices for energy, so crucial to production and shipping costs, have soared, as have vital commodities like copper and steel. And though many of these commodity prices are likely to cool as their bubbles pop or supply catches up to demand, supply chains continue to face pressure from all angles. Meanwhile, attempts by logistics firms to skirt shortages via strategic hoarding have only exacerbated bottlenecks by generating scarcity at other points on the supply chain.

The Great Resignation

Possibly the key bottleneck is the one that has the most potential from the Left's standpoint: labor. The United States is today in the midst of a so-called "Great Resignation," with workers fed up with grim working conditions often gravely exacerbated by the pandemic. As a flurry of recent strikes suggest, this has frequently translated into organized labor activity. There have been more work stoppages in 2021 involving over a thousand workers than 2020, though it still trails significantly behind 2019 levels.

With so few US workers unionized, in many cases strikes do not seem to be a feasible course of action. Far more Americans have simply resigned, emboldened by a tightened labor market. In August alone, 4.3 million people, or 2.9 percent of the workforce, quit their jobs. Low-wage workers, many of them on the front lines during the pandemic, are at the forefront of this mass exodus.

Europe's recovery has also spurred a tight labor market, albeit not on the same scale as the United States. Many central European countries have achieved near full-employment, putting pressure on Western European countries typically reliant on comparably cheaper labor from the ex–Eastern Bloc. While much of the Global North is struggling to find workers, vaccine apartheid means workers in the Global South are significantly more vulnerable to COVID-19, putting pressure on workers in key extraction and production segments of the supply chain.

This labor shortage has also wracked the logistics sector, with shortages of dockworkers and, especially, truckers. The United States is short more than sixty thousand truckers, vital for moving freight from ports to factories for finishing or across the country to warehouses for local distribution. This closing step in the supply chain isn't just struggling in the United States. Europe is in need of four hundred thousand truckers, with Germany alone short eighty thousand.

As with many positions during the Great Resignation, there are actually enough certified truck drivers in the United States. It's just such a brutal job that few people want to do it. Logging crushing hours for low pay, port truckers are typically classified as independent contractors, with few benefits and protections, forced to purchase their own equipment and compete with one another as atomized small businesses. This work looks particularly unattractive amidst the pandemic, especially as workers have a bit of leverage and can change fields. Trucking wasn't always like this:

drivers were typically standard employees until regulatory shifts in the 1980s made reclassification possible.

That working conditions for truckers have eroded even as their labor became a more vital part of the global economy is no coincidence: it's part of a global race to the bottom caused by the so-called "logistics revolution." The elements that make the entire system so vulnerable were seen as positives, until a crisis of this magnitude entered the picture.

Just-Too-Late?

Labor deregulations beginning in the 1970s and evolutions in transportation technology paved the way for today's supply chain capitalism. The logistics revolution converged production and distribution into a single, comprehensive system of design, production, warehousing, sale, and circulation of goods to maximize profits.

Managing a cohesive system of production enabled companies to respond immediately to market fluctuations and squeeze profitability out of every step of the supply chain. Usually sold as boosting efficiency, this almost always came at the expense of workers' wages, conditions, and power, regardless of their role in the process. This boosted profits tremendously; but the system is proving less durable in the face of today's extreme market fluctuations.

The goal was to link supply and demand and eliminate friction between the two, conceptualizing the supply chain as a single system meant to continuously flow at all times. This is contingent on flexible, "just-in-time" production, where goods are produced on-demand, often with inputs at varying points on the now globalized process, to prevent overproduction. Why pay for goods to sit in depots when container ships can serve as floating warehouses and goods can immediately be moved on after arrival, ensuring the coveted one-day shipping?

Less friction might mean everything runs faster—but the flexibility that was once seen as the logistics sector's greatest asset is now coming back to haunt it. Given that storing surpluses of goods is seen as antithetical to modern production and that maintaining an increasingly elaborate, world-spanning system drives capitalism, it shouldn't be a surprise that a global pandemic ravaging supply, concurrent with tectonic shifts in demand, might cast this nimble system into crisis. Supply chains are doing exactly what they're supposed to: agile flexibility is king, and agile flexibility is by default not robust.

The global nature of supply chains—pitting workers globally against each other, under constant threat of capital flight—has typically allowed manufacturers to circumvent crises. Constant circulation and interchangeable production meant a hiccup at one point of the supply chain could simply be avoided. Finish the product in Mexico, not Taiwan, import it in Oakland, not Long Beach, etc.

Logistics firms have further committed to flexibilizing their supply chains in the wake of the pandemic, with many developing "China plus one" strategies to ensure they're not overly dependent on Chinese production. Now, though, every link is on fire, and backups or breakouts in China or the United States help slow down the whole system. This is a direct result of a system that can get a TV shipped to your door in less than twenty-four hours from nearly anywhere in the world.

Hammering the Weak Links?

The supply chain crisis hasn't just frustrated holiday shoppers, or presented more serious challenges, like pushing heating costs for families or producing shortages in medical supplies. It's helped prove the theory, long pushed by Marxist geographers, that supply chains are capitalism's weak links.

For over a decade, names such as Kim Moody and Jake Alimahomed-Wilson have argued that the transition to a global, flexible supply chain under the logistics revolution has created vulnerable choke points capable of pressuring, or even stopping, global capitalism. Full disclosure: I, too, have made this argument.

The current crisis has borne out the notion that these chokepoints are vulnerable targets.

Unfortunately, instead of this bringing hope to theorists and organizers in the logistics space, this crisis should give us pause. Yes, a spanner has been thrown in the works of global capitalism. But considering that a horrendous pandemic, still raging largely unchecked in most of the world, originated in the planet's industrial center—intermittently grounding life to a halt for much of the world's population—this crisis hasn't exactly brought key players in the logistics sector to their knees, as shippers and retailers amass record profits. And though it's hard to know for sure, there are signs indicating the crisis is already easing.

While we finally have evidence of the widespread vulnerability of supply chains, seeing just what it takes to seriously hurt them is an unsavory taste of reality for workers. Simply put, organized labor is nowhere near capable of putting a dent in the supply chain. Though most of those on the Left that call for exploiting the weak points in global capitalism generated by the logistics revolution are earnest about what a challenge this would be, the pandemic has demonstrated that a staggering crisis is required to make an impact. Labor has struggled to take advantage of this moment, and seems incapable of replicating a similarly serious challenge to the supply chain anytime soon.

While the hallmark of the supply chain crisis, overloaded container ships floating idly, waiting to deliver their wares, has materialized most remarkably in the United States, American labor is uniquely under-equipped to lead a global workers movement. With a union density of roughly 10 percent (and an even worse 6.3 percent in the private sector), organized labor in the United States is especially weak, even in the context of recent militant, headline-grabbing strikes.

Though organized labor's implosion in the United States might have been more drastic than most other countries, it represents a broader trend. The average union density in OECD countries is just 15.8 percent, down from 20.9 percent in 2000. Though longshoremen jobs in western ports are often unionized, it's usually a very different story for other positions along the supply chain, from resource extraction to assembly and delivery via ship, train, and truck.

The shifts brought on by the logistic revolution's deregulation and emphasis on flexible production have almost always further atomized workers, ensuring that even as more sectors of the economy are sucked into supply chains, actually organizing these workers has gotten tougher. While the crisis should be a golden opportunity for labor, the changes that have created glaring weak spots in the global economy have also made it harder for increasingly nonunionized, subcontracted, and disconnected workers to leverage their dwindling power.

It's not just a question of union density (or worker militancy, which doesn't directly translate into union membership). Successfully challenging global capitalism means successfully coordinating workers' movements internationally, adding another layer to the task. Usually, an overloaded port or occupied factory is simply bypassed for the next-closest option. It's only now that nearly every port is overloaded and production has been halted at factories in entire regions, that we've seen tremors sent through the entire system.

Centralization in the sector means a few key firms have massive targets on their backs. Yet, their size and resources have helped them eviscerate unionization attempts. This is especially true of two US-based retailers that have helped drive the logistics revolution: Walmart and Amazon. The shift to just-in-time production reshaped the power balance away from manufacturers toward retailers, as goods are now produced so quickly that retailers can dictate exactly how much of and when a product is manufactured.

Walmart's early adoption of just-in-time production allowed it to undercut competition and squeeze workers along the supply chain. The United States' largest employer, it is now so influential on production it can fine suppliers for late—or even early!—deliveries. Amazon took Walmart's model and adapted it to the digital age, and has only become more vital to the United States and world economy in the wake of the pandemic. Both have evolved from retailers to pivotal logistics firms in the global economy.

None of Walmart's 1.6 million US employees are unionized (despite nearly two decades in labor's crosshairs) and Amazon has proven equally adept at union-busting. While these retailers have outsized influence, labor has most frequently challenged them either at the point of sale or at distribution centers, toward the end of the supply chain where targets are most diffuse and easiest to circumvent.

Hurting them further up the supply chain would mean not just challenging two of the biggest, most ruthless companies on earth, it would mean organizing workers typically classified as independent contractors or employed by subcontracting firms. Despite their concentration on paper, they're more thinly spread where it matters for labor—in their workplaces.

[…]

VIEWPOINT 2

> "The most vulnerable people in society have been the first and hardest hit."

The Pandemic Revealed Supply Chain Failures
Chloé Farand

In this viewpoint, Chloé Farand explores how shocks on the supply chain immediately impact the movement of essential goods—namely food—around the world. Turning to the example of the COVID-19 pandemic, she takes stock of crops that were allowed to go bad in warehouses around the world, due to sudden declines in immediate demand. This reflected a failure of supply chain design, she writes, as rampant starvation plagued some parts of the world while food rotted in the west. Chloé Farand is a writer at Climate Home News, a London news outlet that focuses on climate issues.

As you read, consider the following questions:

1. How do issues with supply chain management translate to issues with distributing food around the world?
2. What's one possible solution to simplifying essential supply chains to make them more resilient to shocks?
3. How do export restrictions impact the price of food around the world?

"Shorter Supply Chains Needed to End Hunger After Pandemic: UN Envoy," by Chloé Farand, Climate Home News Ltd, May 15, 2020. Reprinted by permission.

The coronavirus crisis is deepening inequalities in accessing healthy food, the UN special envoy for food systems has warned.

As governments imposed trade and travel restrictions to curb the spread of Covid-19, global supply chains have been disrupted, hindering the distribution of food from farms to consumers largely concentrated in urban areas.

Meanwhile the economic slowdown has triggered a fall in demand, leaving unsellable fruits and vegetables rotting in fields and orchards and farmers without an income.

"My biggest concern is that there are a whole load of people out there that had the ability to feed themselves and now can't," Agnes Kalibata, of Rwanda, said. It puts the UN sustainable development goal to eradicate hunger by 2030 further out of reach.

Developing shorter supply chains where possible to get food to those who need it and reduce the sector's environmental impact will be important, Kalibata said.

In December last year, Kalibata was appointed by UN Secretary General António Guterres to lead a Food Systems Summit in the second half of 2021.

The event, due to be attended by governments, businesses and experts, is designed to create momentum around transforming the global food system to meet the 2030 Sustainable Development Goals and ensure people have access to healthy diets while protecting the planet.

The coronavirus outbreak has brought the summit's objectives into sharp focus, exposing the weaknesses of food production, processing and distribution as millions are now faced with starvation.

The most vulnerable people in society have been the first and hardest hit, Kalibata told Climate Home News in a video call.

"This is the group of people that is having to make choices around nutrition and how many times a day they eat. It is becoming increasingly clear that the strain on household nutrition is going to become the biggest impact of the crisis," she said.

Before the Covid-19 outbreak, UN agencies were already forecasting acute food insecurity for 2020 driven by conflicts in Yemen and Central Africa and the Middle East, an outbreak of desert locusts in East Africa, extreme weather events in the Caribbean, adverse climate in the Sahel and West Africa and socio-political crisis and high food prices in Latin America.

Last month, the World Food Programme (WFP) estimated the pandemic had doubled the number of people that could face acute food insecurity by the end of 2020 to 265 million people.

David Beasley, executive director of the WFP, said millions of people faced being pushed to the brink of starvation, warning of a "hunger pandemic."

"If we don't prepare and act now—to secure access, avoid funding shortfalls and disruptions to trade—we could be facing multiple famines of biblical proportions within a short few months," he said.

"The knee jerk reaction is to be inward looking, to secure our borders and our food," Kalibata said.

According to Unctad, the UN body dealing with trade, global trade is projected to fall by a record 27% in the second quarter of the year. And 21 countries have responded to the pandemic with export restrictions, according to the International Food Policy Research Institute.

Kalibata warned that governments turning their backs on global trade and imposing export restrictions risked increasing food prices, fearing a repeat of the 2007/8 food price spike.

"I don't think global trade is a weakness," she said, pointing out that many countries don't have the capacity to produce enough nutritious food to feed their population.

But the development of shorter supply chains that can channel perishable and nutritious food quicker and with less environmental impact, will be critical, she added.

From farm to fork, the food supply chain accounts for 29% of global greenhouse gas emissions, according to the UN. About a third of all food produced goes to waste.

Supplying the Fight Against Hunger

SA Harvest is taking a revolutionary approach in the pursuit to end hunger in South Africa by exposing flaws in the current food ecosystem. Further, they are creating a food rescue initiative.

Leading logistics companies have responded with speed and generosity to help food rescue organisation SA Harvest to address hunger and devastation.

These include Waterford Carriers from Johannesburg and Time Link Cargo from Cape Town, along with additional logistical support from Bex Carriers and Bulldog Hauliers. "Their contribution is incalculable and made the provision of over 90 tons of food, toiletries, baby food, nappies and other essentials possible within a matter of days," says SA Harvest CEO Alan Browde.

SA Harvest's response to the rioting and looting began immediately as the severity of the damage and the growing shortages became evident. Since launching in September 2019, SA Harvest has built up a strong infrastructure, logistical and technology capabilities, and was therefore able to respond immediately and efficiently.

SA Harvest was established in 2019 when around 14 million people were going hungry every day. Since then, the need has increased due to the extended lockdown and consequent increase in unemployment to unprecedented levels.

The organisation is taking a revolutionary approach to ending hunger by addressing its systemic root causes, leveraging innovative technology, and simultaneously tackling the immediate need through rescuing nutritious food that would have gone to waste and delivering it where it's needed most.

SA Harvest has a fleet of refrigerated and other vehicles operating from warehouses in Briardene in Durban, Epping in Cape Town and Sandton in Johannesburg. A proprietary technology platform is being built to enhance the organisation's logistics capability, which will help enhance the efficiency of the entire food rescue supply chain. Browde says, "this platform will allow for knowledge and data sharing with NGOs and other key stakeholders and bring about the collaboration needed to build solutions. It empowers how we tackle the problem of food waste in South Africa and eventually scale sufficiently for our industry to be more effective."

"Supply Chain Companies to Join the Fight Against Hunger," by Dhiyora Naidoo, SCN Africa, September 7, 2021.

While local food systems are not going to replace the global food trade, the creation of new intra-regional markets could plug the demand gap during the pandemic and global recession that follows.

Across Africa, south east Asia, Latin America and the Caribbean region, current levels of regional trade are very low, Jamie Morrison, director of the Food Systems Programme at the Food and Agriculture Organisation (FAO), told CHN.

Many African countries are reliant on export commodities such as coffee, tea and tropical fruits, for example. Increasing the consumption of these commodities in Africa would support local economies while building resilience in the food system.

"The development of regional markets could also have a positive impact on food loss from supply chains, which could be less susceptible to perishability issues," Morrison said. Shorter supply chains could also limit the need for energy-intensive refrigeration, which is expected to rise as the planet heats up.

The pandemic has also put the link between nutrition, health and development into sharp relief.

While the number of hungry people is on the rise, reaching 820 million over the past three years, about two billion people are overweight or obese and 30% of all deaths are linked to nutrition-related diseases, said Kalibata.

The 2020 Global Nutrition Report published this week highlighted the link between inequities in the food system and health inequalities.

While undernourished people have a weaker immune system and can be at greater risks of the virus, people with obesity and diabetes have been found to be more likely to die from Covid-19.

"There is a real risk that, as nations strive to control the virus, the gains they have made in reducing hunger and malnutrition will be lost," the report warned.

It found that shorter supply chains for fresh food delivery to the most nutritionally disadvantaged could help address nutrition imbalance.

As governments work out recovery packages to the pandemic's economic impact, the Food and Land Use Coalition called for investment into diversifying food supply chains and developing regional food systems to build resilience.

For the next 18 months, UN special envoy Kalibata will be working to create consensus for what a future sustainable food system should look like. Supply chains, nutrition, education, waste and climate change are all issues to be addressed by the summit.

"It will require countries to commit to do things differently. We need to be concerned about having a healthy planet and healthy people living on this planet—addressing that is a huge undertaking," she said.

VIEWPOINT 3

> "It appears that we are now headed in the direction blazed by the East German economy, not toward the status quo ante."

Why Don't Supply Chain Problems Occur More Often?

Walter Block

In the following viewpoint Walter Block argues that the COVID-related supply chain issues are an anomaly thanks to free enterprise. The author describes how the citizens of communist East Germany did not understand the extent to which their leaders restricted their supply of goods and claims that the United States is undergoing a similar situation at the hands of oppressive government regulation. Walter Block holds the Harold E. Wirth Eminent Scholar Endowed Chair in Economics at the J. A. Butt School of Business at Loyola University New Orleans. He is a member of the FEE Faculty Network.

As you read, consider the following questions:

1. Why does the author compare supply chain issues in the United States to East Germany?
2. What is Adam Smith's "Invisible Hand"?
3. What blame does the viewpoint lay on President Biden?

"What East Germany Can Teach Americans about the Current Supply Chain Crisis," by Walter Block, Foundation for Economic Education, January 20, 2022, https://fee.org/articles/what-east-germany-can-teach-americans-about-the-current-supply-chain-crisis/. Licensed under CC BY 4.0.

Global Trade and the Supply Chain

What is happening with our supply chains? They seem very rusty, if not altogether broken. There are numerous ships at several California ports waiting patiently to be unloaded. We are talking thousands, maybe tens of thousands, of gigantic railroad car sized containers, all just sitting there; well, floating there. Meanwhile, our supermarket shelves are sometimes as much as half empty. Grocers are all too often out of the foodstuffs and other things we used to take for granted.

A similar situation took place a while ago. Supermarkets in West Germany were chock full of products. In East Germany? Not at all. The communist functionaries who visited West Germany (there were two Germanies after World War Two) complained that only a few grocery stores in East Germany were as fully packed as those in West Germany. They assumed that the Western powers were selectively showing them the better grocery stores just to (falsely) demonstrate the supposed benefits of capitalism. The eastern apparatchiks knew, they just knew, that most other such big box stores in the West had massive amounts of shelves gathering dust, just like the grocery stores in the East.

This tactic would not have been new. In medieval times, when a city was under siege, starved of food, the defenders would still gorge a few people; they were kept fat to show the surrounding army that their tactics were a failure. The capitalists in West Germany were accused by the communists of East Germany of analogous "piling on" behavior.

Of course, the communists were all wrong. The West Germans, like participants in all other countries where free enterprise was not entirely smothered, had full shelves everywhere. Profit and loss considerations ensured this. It was not a special ploy to show up the Communists, it was just an everyday occurrence.

The problem in West Germany and all other such nations, in the view of some, was that it had too many goods, too many choices. For example, Senator Bernie Sanders continually complains about there being too many brands of breakfast cereal, toothpaste, and deodorant. Maybe Bernie would be happier in countries like

Venezuela, nowadays, where the "problem" of a surfeit of goods does not exist. Certainly, this problem would not have plagued him if he lived in East Germany after World War Two. (Come to think of it, he did spend his "honeymoon" in the USSR.)

Until the Biden administration, all our large groceries, and small ones too, were bursting at the seams. It appears that we are now headed in the direction blazed by the East German economy, not toward the status quo ante.

Forget for a moment supply chain problems. They are unusual. Why, ordinarily, do they not occur, at least not in countries with a bit more than vestigial free enterprise institutions? It is simple: free market prices, the profit and loss system, private property rights.

Consider this simplified supply chain. 1. The farmer grows wheat. It is shipped to 2. the commercial baker. That firm combines material from this crop with yeast, salt, milk, and other such ingredients of bread. This product next appears in the 3. grocery store. Initially the profits earned by all three are equal at 5%. Thus, there is no tendency for resources to shift anywhere; everything stays put—we are at equilibrium.

But then let us suppose something comes up to disturb this idyllic scenario. Posit that some of the baker's ovens go out of order due to overheating. He can only use half as many inputs as before, and, thus, now ship out, say, half as many loaves. The price of wheat falls since he is purchasing less from the farmer. The price of bread rises, since he is now supplying less to the retailer. Profits in baking rise from both these sources.

But profits under free enterprise are like a call in the wilderness from a lost hiker in the woods. With high baking profits, other bakers expand their base of operation. They put on extra shifts and are led by Adam Smith's "Invisible Hand" (he thought this was the hand of God) to do something in their selfish interest, earn more profit, which just also happens, providentially, to be in the public good. (Ronald Reagan, bless him, called this the "magic of the market.")

As a result of this tugging, pulling, and pushing of the free marketplace, more wheat is now purchased from farmers, raising its price, and thus reducing the baker's profit. Also, more bread now heads in the direction of the consumer, thus lowering prices and thus profits in baking. We are back to normal once again. (Homework: trace through what would happen if farmers lost half their crop due to a frost; show which market forces would bring us back to an even keel; hey, I'm a professor, I have to give homework, or they'll kick me out of the profession).

So, why is this automatic profit and loss system failing us?

In no small part due to the Biden administration's policies, we no longer have as much of a laissez faire capitalist system as once prevailed. The profits that once attracted entrepreneurs have been impeded with tax and regulatory hurdles, and the president's misguided policies have helped create a historic labor shortage, leaving many productive workers on the sidelines. Mr. Biden for many months paid people as much or more for sitting on their couches as they could have earned working, so it's no wonder that all too few people are flooding into trucking, or baking and farming in the hypothetical example.

Then, too, Mr. Trump's efforts to reduce regulation have been overcome by the present White House. For example, truckers in California have been made to jump through extra hoops. (Trump's support of lockdowns is another matter; they have no doubt created significant problems throughout the pandemic.)

Fortunately, the solution to the supply chain crisis is not complex. Supermarkets in West Germany were packed with goods because its leaders allowed for a relatively free market. Their counterparts across the Berlin Wall failed because they believed they could effectively regulate an economy.

If America wishes to avoid the fate of the East Germans, it should abandon interventionist policies and recognize that prosperity lies in a laissez faire capitalist system.

VIEWPOINT 4

> "So long as globalization was driven by freer movement in goods, services and capital, educated and skilled workers in developed and developing countries would benefit, while unskilled workers in developing countries would gain at the expense of unskilled workers in developed countries."

Globalization Is Undergoing a Course Correction

Rohinton Medhora

In the following viewpoint, Rohinton Medhora addresses the question that has subsequently underpinned a lot of the discussion over how globalization was impacted by COVID-19: will it ever reverse? Will the world ever become less globalized than it is right now? Medhora says no and, in fact, argues that any sign that people are looking at the issue differently is a good thing. It means globalization is doing better than ever. Rohinton Medhora has written and edited various books about globalization and is president of the Centre for International Governance Innovation, a Canadian think tank founded by the former CEO of the company behind the Blackberry brand.

"Is Globalization in Reverse?" by Rohinton Medhora, Gateway House Indian Council on Global Relations, February 8, 2017. This article was published by Gateway House. Reprinted by permission.

Global Trade and the Supply Chain

As you read, consider the following questions:

1. What were some of the events that pointed to the power of populist rhetoric in the political landscape of modern democracies around the world?
2. Why is globalization considered "a hard sell," by some economists?
3. According to the viewpoint, what is the real wild card in predicting how globalization develops?

Is globalization in reverse? The question animates discussion. The evidence is mixed at best, and does not warrant some of the more dire scenarios [1] being bruited about. But globalization's contours are changing, and this is not a bad thing.

The Brexit vote and the election of Donald Trump are presented as Exhibits A and B of the manifestation of a change in public attitudes to globalization. These votes did show the power of populist electioneering, much of it having a strong anti-global tinge to it. But in Brexit, turnout by age and socio-economic characteristics played a crucial role [2] in the final result. Turnout was high among older and non-urban voters and low among younger urban ones. Had the turnout been reversed, the results would have been different.

In the case of the United States election, President Donald Trump lost the popular vote by almost three million votes. Besides, not all votes for his ticket reflected anti-global tendencies just as not all votes for the Hillary Clinton ticket embodied pro-global sentiments. The electoral college system magnified what was a qualified victory into a seemingly overwhelming one. Neither the British nor the U.S. votes suggest a large change in underlying attitudes to globalization.

Other smaller, but no less troubling, instances currently cited, such as elections in Hungary and the Philippines, appear to be driven as much by domestic considerations as by perceptions about the world writ large. There are important unknowns about what the continued strength or ascension of leaders in China, India and Russia signifies. While each of them, and especially President Xi Jinping and Prime Minister Narendra Modi, has espoused nationalist rhetoric, they have also embarked upon a series of ventures that project their countries overseas and craft a global strategy that is premised on the very tenets of globalization —trade, and more generally economics first, international alliances, and an eye to making the best of the information age. How else do we explain Prime Minister Modi's visits to 45 countries, (many of them repeat visits) and the resulting accords? China is on nothing less than a global tear, with the creation of the Asian Infrastructure Investment Bank, Silk Road Initiative, Regional Comprehensive Economic Partnership and positioning itself [3] as (at least) half of a "G2".

Such multi-country surveys [4] as there are suggest that support for globalization, especially its economic aspects, is stronger in emerging countries than in developed countries, and that attitudes towards it are more positive among young people than older ones. But on political and social issues, such differences disappear, or at least require nuance [5] in interpretation. We must recognize that the sample size of such surveys is minuscule and seldom representative of the population as a whole, and that we do not have enough of a time series in the results to discern trends.

The broad storyline of support for globalization in developing countries (especially the larger ones) and scepticism about it in developed countries is consistent with the underlying economics. Writing in 1995, Adrian Wood was among the first to present globalization as it was likely to unfold [6], and its implications. To wit, so long as globalization was driven by freer movement in goods, services and capital, educated and skilled workers in developed and developing countries would benefit, while unskilled workers in developing countries would gain at the expense of unskilled workers in developed countries. When coupled with the lack of compensating [7] retraining, safety net and other social policies in developed countries (especially the U.S. and U.K.), the resulting backlash was predictable.

Globalization, particularly in trade, has always been a hard sell [8]. The International Trade Organization, proposed at Bretton Woods in 1944, never got off the ground because of opposition in many countries' legislatures, especially in the U.S. It wasn't until 1995 that the World Trade Organization came into being. By then, the GATT Rounds had lowered tariffs to the point where only the tough nuts—like agriculture and a host of "behind the border" issues like competition and investment policy—remained, grinding multilateral global trade negotiations to a crawl.

What next? As the contours of globalization are reshaped, a pause might seem like reversal. It isn't; the pause might even be desirable. The globalization of the past three decades has been unbalanced—high in movement of finance and the spread of information and communications technologies; medium in trade in goods and services; and low in movement of people and the development of regulatory and other policy responses at the national and supranational levels. If the pause is about, at the very least, managing global capital movement more sensibly, developing regimes to promote green technologies and their spread, building up an arsenal of domestic social policies [9], and, more broadly, creating a national consensus around a country's place in the world, then it will be time well spent.

Meanwhile, there is one wild card that no one appears to control. Technological change in areas come to be known as the fourth industrial revolution [10] proceeds apace. We do not know all the risks and opportunities that this movement presents, and—crucially—to whom they will present themselves. But technology is at least as powerful a driver of economic change [11]—and vitally, job displacement—as government policy is. In the absence of a clear sense about this trend, policy responses will either be non-existent or imperfect. The seeds of a reaction to the next wave of globalization are already being sown, and it too will seem mistakenly like reversal.

References

[1] Barbieri, Pierpaolo, "The Losers of Deglobalization," Foreign Affairs, 13 November 2016, https://www.foreignaffairs.com/articles/2016-11-13/losers-deglobalization

[2] Burn-Murdoch, John, "Brexit: voter turnout by age," Financial Times, 24 June 2016 http://blogs.ft.com/ftdata/2016/06/24/loomb-demographic-divide-eu-referendum-results/

[3] Xi, Jingpin, "Opening Plenary at Davos 2017," speech delivered at Davos, 17 January 2017, https://www.weforum.org/agenda/2017/01/full-text-of-xi-jinping-keynote-at-the-world-economic-forum (Accessed on 8 February 2017)

[4] "What the world thinks about Globalization," The Economist, 18 November 2016, http://www.economist.com/blogs/graphicdetail/2016/11/daily-chart-12

[5] "Faith and Skepticism about Trade, Foreign Investment," Pew Research Center, 16 September 2014, http://www.pewglobal.org/2014/09/16/faith-and-skepticism-about-trade-foreign-investment/

[6] Wood, Adrian, "North-South Trade, Employment and Inequality: Changing Fortunes in a Skill-Driven World," Oxford University Press, 1995

[7] Atkinson, Anthony B., "Is Rising Inequality Inevitable? A Critique of the Transatlantic Consensus," United Nations University, November 1999, https://www.wider.unu.edu/sites/default/files/AL03-1999.pdf

[8] Medhora, Rohinton P., "Refreshing Global Trade Governance," Council of Councils, 19 January 2017, http://www.cfr.org/councilofcouncils/global_memos/p38685

[9] Daniels, Ronald J., Michael Trebilcock, "A Better Way to Help U.S. Victims of Free Trade," Bloomberg, 2 December 2016, https://www.bloomberg.com/view/articles/2016-12-02/a-better-way-to-help-u-s-victims-of-free-trade

[10] Schwab, Klaus, "The Fourth Industrial Revolution," World Economic Forum, January 2016, http://www3.weforum.org/docs/Media/KSC_4IR.pdf

[11] Rotman, David, "How Technology Is Destroying Jobs," MIT Technology Review, 12 June 2013, https://www.technologyreview.com/s/515926/how-technology-is-destroying-jobs/

Periodical and Internet Sources Bibliography

The following articles have been selected to supplement the diverse views presented in this chapter.

Madeleine Davies, "The Most Interesting Oil in the World," Eater, December 9, 2021, https://www.eater.com/22824431/history-globalization-environmental-impact-palm-oil.

Renee Dubiel, "Gen Z is going to reinvent the supply chain," Fast Company, April 28 2022, https://www.fastcompany.com/90743143/gen-z-is-going-to-reinvent-the-supply-chain.

Peter S. Goodman, "This Is What Happens When Globalization Breaks Down," *New York Times*, March 31, 2022, https://www.nytimes.com/2022/03/31/business/supply-chain-small-business.html.

Rebecca Heilweil, "The history of the metal box that's wrecking the supply chain," Vox, December 14, 2021, https://www.vox.com/recode/22832884/shipping-containers-amazon-supply-chain.

Diana Hubbell, "There Has Been Blood," Eater, August 3, 2021, https://www.eater.com/22589445/palm-oil-thailand-plantation-spft-jiew-kang-jue-pattana.

Yasaman Kazemi, "How The Modern Supply Chain Is Evolving," *Forbes*, June 27, 2019, https://www.forbes.com/sites/yasamankazemi/2019/06/27/how-the-modern-supply-chain-is-evolving/?sh=6c6784b169b2.

Jacques Leslie, "How climate change is disrupting the global supply chain," Yale Environment 360, March 10, 2022, https://e360.yale.edu/features/how-climate-change-is-disrupting-the-global-supply-chain.

Scott Mall, "Malcom McLean's container ship begins first journey in 1956," FreightWaves, April 26, 2022, https://www.freightwaves.com/news/freightwaves-classics-malcom-mcdowells-containership-begins-first-journey-in-1956.

Sean Mueller, "The China Equation: How One Country's Supply Chain Affects All Others," Symbia Third Party Logistics, October 22, 2021, https://www.symbia.com/resources/china-equation-countrys-supply-chain-affects-all-others.

Peer Schouten, "How Literal Roadblocks Hinder the Supply Chain," *Wall Street Journal*, April 21, 2022, wsj.com/articles/preventing-supply-chain-extortion-terrorism-jihadist-islamist-isis-rebels-heineken-ericsson-sanctions-iraq-congo-warzone-conflict-zone-11650474876.

Kandy Wong and He Huifeng, "China's manufacturers remain key to global supply chain, producers 'even more dependent' on world's factory," *South China Morning Post*, April 29, 2022, https://www.scmp.com/economy/china-economy/article/3175865/chinas-manufacturers-remain-key-global-supply-chain-producers.

OPPOSING VIEWPOINTS® SERIES

CHAPTER 3

Can Trade Policy Be Used Effectively?

Chapter Preface

Trade policy describes the ways that countries use the power of their borders to control what enters and what leaves the self-contained economic unit of the nation state. Supply chains look at how items get from place to place; trade policies regulate those goods once they are inside the borders of another country.

In an immediate way, the tools used in trade policy reflect ways of politically negotiating the impacts of globalization. If products that are imported from some countries are too cheap to sustain a domestic economy, using tariffs can be seen as a way to level the playing field. If two countries have become economically codependent or share similar economic goals, a trade agreement can help develop a bloc of like-minded trading partners. Economic ties, of course, are apt to become political ones: the European Union, a political body that consists of multiple houses of parliament, started out as a trade group called the European Coal and Steel Community.

One of the central tensions that the following viewpoints convey is the disparate conflict between free trade policies, which are largely supported by most mainstream economists around the world, and the more heavy-handed approach that's often promised by political leaders. Voters, especially in countries that regularly conduct elections, want to see their elected officials take a more active role in determining what kinds of goods fill up the marketplace. Economists, however, tend to think the wide-scale impact of these kinds of decisions is minimal, and the main losers of these policies are the very consumers who supported them.

No large country in the world is self-sufficient. Goods are constantly needed to fill stores and provide the standard of living that citizens are used to. In this chapter, you will read viewpoints that have cast their lot with the future of globalized growth, while others are warier of the repercussions that could have.

VIEWPOINT 1

> "Except in cases in which the costs of production do not include such social costs as pollution, the world is better off when countries import products that are produced more efficiently in other countries."

What's So Free About Trade?

Brad McDonald

In the following viewpoint, Brad McDonald draws on a central contradiction between how economists look at free trade and how ordinary people do. He writes that economists consider free trade to be the most efficient way to distribute goods, and thus it is a very good thing. On the other hand, consumers consider these new items a strange addition to their common marketplace. This sets up a recurring tension in trade policy, which is often split between the needs of its central players and everyone else. Brad McDonald is an executive at the International Monetary Fund, an international banking group.

As you read, consider the following questions:

1. Why is "free trade" generally unpopular in almost every country?
2. What are some of the instinctive reasons that countries trade?
3. What do trade barriers seek to accomplish?

"International Trade: Commerce Among Nations," by Brad McDonald, The International Monetary Fund, February 24, 2020. Reprinted by permission.

If there is a point on which most economists agree, it is that trade among nations makes the world better off. Yet international trade can be one of the most contentious of political issues, both domestically and between governments.

When a firm or an individual buys a good or a service produced more cheaply abroad, living standards in both countries increase. There are other reasons consumers and firms buy abroad that also make them better off—the product may better fit their needs than similar domestic offerings or it may not be available domestically. In any case, the foreign producer also benefits by making more sales than it could selling solely in its own market and by earning foreign exchange (currency) that can be used by itself or others in the country to purchase foreign-made products.

Still, even if societies as a whole gain when countries trade, not every individual or company is better off. When a firm buys a foreign product because it is cheaper, it benefits—but the (more costly) domestic producer loses a sale. Usually, however, the buyer gains more than the domestic seller loses. Except in cases in which the costs of production do not include such social costs as pollution, the world is better off when countries import products that are produced more efficiently in other countries.

Those who perceive themselves to be affected adversely by foreign competition have long opposed international trade. Soon after economists such as Adam Smith and David Ricardo established the economic basis for free trade, British historian Thomas B. Macaulay was observing the practical problems governments face in deciding whether to embrace the concept: "Free trade, one of the greatest blessings which a government can confer on a people, is in almost every country unpopular."

Two centuries later trade debates still resonate.

Why Countries Trade

In one of the most important concepts in economics, Ricardo observed that trade was driven by comparative rather than absolute costs (of producing a good). One country may be more productive than others in all goods, in the sense that it can produce any good using fewer inputs (such as capital and labor) than other countries require to produce the same good. Ricardo's insight was that such a country would still benefit from trading according to its comparative advantage—exporting products in which its absolute advantage was greatest, and importing products in which its absolute advantage was comparatively less (even if still positive).

Though a country may be twice as productive as its trading partners in making clothing, if it is three times as productive in making steel or building airplanes, it will benefit from making and exporting these products and importing clothes. Its partner will gain by exporting clothes—in which it has a comparative but not absolute advantage—in exchange for these other products. The notion of comparative advantage also extends beyond physical goods to trade in services—such as writing computer code or providing financial products.

Because of comparative advantage, trade raises the living standards of both countries. Douglas Irwin (2009) calls comparative advantage "good news" for economic development. "Even if a developing country lacks an absolute advantage in any field, it will always have a comparative advantage in the production of some goods," and will trade profitably with advanced economies.

Differences in comparative advantage may arise for several reasons. In the early 20th century, Swedish economists Eli Heckscher and Bertil Ohlin identified the role of labor and capital, so-called factor endowments, as a determinant of advantage. The Heckscher-Ohlin proposition maintains that countries tend to export goods whose production uses intensively the factor of production that is relatively abundant in the country. Countries well endowed with capital—such as factories and machinery—should export capital-intensive products, while those well endowed with labor should export labor-intensive products. Economists today think that factor endowments matter, but that there are also other important influences on trade patterns (Baldwin, 2008).

Recent research finds that episodes of trade opening are followed by adjustment not only across industries, but within them as well. The increase in competition coming from foreign firms puts pressure on profits, forcing less efficient firms to contract and making room for more efficient firms. Expansion and new entry bring with them better technologies and new product varieties. Likely the most important is that trade enables greater selection across different types of goods (say refrigerators). This explains why there is a lot of intra-industry trade (for example, countries that export household refrigerators may import industrial coolers), which is something that the factor endowment approach does not encompass.

There are clear efficiency benefits from trade that results in more products—not only more of the same products, but greater product variety. For example, the United States imports four times as many varieties (such as different types of cars) as it did in the 1970s, while the number of countries supplying each good has doubled. An even greater benefit may be the more efficient investment spending that results from firms having access to a wider variety and quality of intermediate and capital inputs (think industrial optical lenses rather than cars). By enhancing overall investment and facilitating innovation, trade can bring sustained higher growth.

Indeed, economic models used to assess the impact of trade typically neglect influences involving technology transfer and pro-competitive forces such as the expansion of product varieties. That is because these influences are difficult to model, and results that do incorporate them are subject to greater uncertainty. Where this has been done, however, researchers have concluded that the benefits of trade reforms—such as reducing tariffs and other nontariff barriers to trade—are much larger than suggested by conventional models.

Why Trade Reform Is Difficult

Trade contributes to global efficiency. When a country opens up to trade, capital and labor shift toward industries in which they are used more efficiently. That movement provides society a higher level of economic welfare. However, these effects are only part of the story.

Trade also brings dislocation to those firms and industries that cannot cut it. Firms that face difficult adjustment because of more efficient foreign producers often lobby against trade. So do their workers. They often seek barriers such as import taxes (called tariffs) and quotas to raise the price or limit the availability of imports. Processors may try to restrict the exportation of raw materials to depress artificially the price of their own inputs. By contrast, the benefits of trade are spread diffusely and its beneficiaries often do not recognize how trade benefits them. As a result, opponents are often quite effective in discussions about trade.

Trade Policies

Reforms since World War II have substantially reduced government-imposed trade barriers. But policies to protect domestic industries vary. Tariffs are much higher in certain sectors (such as agriculture and clothing) and among certain country groups (such as less developed countries) than in others. Many countries have substantial barriers to trade in services in areas such as transportation, communications, and, often, the financial sector, while others have policies that welcome foreign competition.

Moreover, trade barriers affect some countries more than others. Often hardest hit are less developed countries, whose exports are concentrated in low-skill, labor-intensive products that industrialized countries often protect. The United States, for example, is reported to collect about 15 cents in tariff revenue for each $1 of imports from Bangladesh (Elliott, 2009), compared with one cent for each $1 of imports from some major western European countries. Yet imports of a particular product from Bangladesh face the same or lower tariffs than do similarly classified products imported from western Europe. Although the tariffs on Bangladesh items in the United States may be a dramatic example, World Bank economists calculated that exporters from low-income countries face barriers on average half again greater than those faced by the exports of major industrialized countries (Kee, Nicita, and Olarreaga, 2006).

The World Trade Organization (WTO) referees international trade. Agreements devised since 1948 by its 153 members (of the WTO and its predecessor General Agreement on Trade and Tariffs) promote nondiscrimination and facilitate further liberalization in nearly all areas of commerce, including tariffs, subsidies, customs valuation and procedures, trade and investment in service sectors, and intellectual property. Commitments under these agreements are enforced through a powerful and carefully crafted dispute settlement process.

Under the rules-based international trading system centered in the WTO, trade policies have become more stable, more transparent, and more open. And the WTO is a key reason why the global financial crisis did not spark widespread protectionism. However, as seen most recently with the Doha Round of WTO trade negotiations, the institution faces big challenges in reaching agreements to open global trade further. Despite successes, restrictive and discriminatory trade policies remain common. Addressing them could yield hundreds of billions of dollars in annual global benefits. But narrow interests have sought to delay and dilute further multilateral reforms. A focus on the greater good, together with ways to help the relatively few that may be adversely affected, can help to deliver a fairer and economically more sensible trading system.

References
Baldwin Robert E., 2008, The Development and Testing of Heckscher-Ohlin Trade Models: A Review, (Cambridge, Massachusetts: MIT Press).
Elliott, Kimberley Ann, 2009, "Opening Markets for Poor Countries: Are We There Yet?" Center for Global Development Working Paper 184 (Washington).
Irwin, Douglas A., 2009, Free Trade under Fire (Princeton, New Jersey: Princeton University Press, 3rd ed.).
Kee, Hiau Looi, Alessandro Nicita, and Marcelo Olarreaga, 2006, "Estimating Trade Restrictiveness Indices," World Bank Policy Research Working Paper No. 3840 (Washington).

VIEWPOINT 2

> "Tariffs and quotas on U.S. imports—including steel—could increase the costs of everything from Christmas presents to energy."

Tariffs Have Negative Effects on U.S. Employment
The Economist

In the following viewpoint, The Economist argues that trade restrictions are harmful, but that most people don't understand the full extent of their impact. It is the economists who know best how to handle trade policy. According to the author, any optimism that consumers generally attribute to economic conditions is actually based on how free trade conditions currently are. Most people, the argument goes, would feel better if those barriers didn't exist at all. The Economist is a British magazine that has published columns on economic issues since 1843.

As you read, consider the following questions:

1. Why don't consumers connect trade policy to the cost of day-to-day items, according to the viewpoint?
2. What negative economic impacts does the viewpoint attribute to trade restrictions?

"The Negative Effects of Tariffs on U.S. Employment," The Economist Newspaper Limited, December 12, 2019. Reproduced courtesy of the American Petroleum Institute.

3. How does the author justify the discrepancies between the popularity of trade restrictions and their grievance with them?

U.S. consumers are feeling optimistic about their future—with unemployment at its lowest levels in years, energy prices lower than last season, and a robust economy. This is due in part to the U.S.' role as a global energy and innovation leader, which allows consumers more disposable income due to lower energy costs. But in the face of ongoing trade wars and tariffs and quotas still in place on imported goods that could cost U.S. jobs and hurt key U.S. energy and manufacturing projects, will consumers' optimism endure?

Generally, while consumers feel good about the U.S. economy, and seem to be less educated about the direct impact of tariffs and quotas, the U.S. business community is taking immediate actions to protect itself from the costly trade wars. For instance, Harley Davidson announced this summer that it would move some production overseas due to EU retaliatory tariffs. In October, Ford prepared for layoffs after the tariffs reportedly cost the company $1bn. GM said in November it will close plants and cut jobs as a result of a sales slowdown and high costs due in part to steel tariffs. Numerous small businesses, too, are endangered by the trade war with China, as are America's farmers. Trade disputes could cost billions of dollars to the agricultural sector, says Farmers for Free Trade, a nonprofit that mobilizes farmers and ranchers to take action to support and expand exports.

Tariffs and quotas on U.S imports—including steel—could increase the costs of everything from Christmas presents to energy. U.S. natural gas and oil production is surging, and new infrastructure like pipelines and export terminals are needed to bring this energy to U.S. and global markets. Restrictions on the availability of imported steel can stop or slow U.S. energy infrastructure projects, which in turn could put upward pressure on the cost of U.S. energy, and therefore increase the costs of manufactured goods and threaten U.S. jobs.

This disconnect between U.S. consumers' general optimism and the negative impacts of trade restrictions on U.S. businesses can be traced to the macro-labor effects of trade policy. Consumers understand the tariffs will eventually hurt their wallets. However, they don't make the leap to how tariffs could also hurt their paychecks. "Because these kinds of tariffs or trade restraints are often hidden, consumers realize higher prices for things will cause them to not purchase as much," says Laura Baughman, president at Trade Partnership Worldwide, a trade and economic consulting firm. "But they don't realize that cuts in purchasing ripple through the economy in all kinds of ways to the point that people lose jobs in sectors they can't even imagine. You can't see it as directly."

Cease-Fire Uncertainty

When the U.S. and China announced a postponement of additional tariffs at the G20 summit in December, it initially felt like good news. Markets rallied; businesses breathed a sigh of relief. The calm, however, was short-lived, as realization set in that the news amounted to a cease-fire, not an actual peace agreement. Both countries put the escalation of the trade war on hold, but did not end it or agree to dismantle existing barriers—including the U.S.'s Section 301 tariffs on a variety of goods from China, and the associated retaliatory tariffs from China on U.S. goods. Plus, consumers are also dealing with the effects from the already implemented U.S. Section 232 tariffs and quotas on imported steel and aluminum from every country except Australia. What is worrisome is that this on-again-off-again uncertainty is just as much of an impediment to trade as tariffs, says Katheryn Russ, associate professor of economics at University of California, Davis and research associate at National Bureau of Economic Research.

"Uncertainty can act like tariffs," says Ms. Russ. "It's still on the table for an extra three months, and we don't know how it will be resolved or how long it will take afterwards—if it's resolved. That's still damaging enough to slow down trade and the overall economy. These tariffs are basically death by a thousand cuts. It's a little bit here, a little bit there. The cumulative effect across everything can really add up."

That's certainly true for Robert Heiblim, the owner of three small consumer technology businesses, one of which was directly hit with 25% tariffs. "Uncertainty is a big enemy of growth and business," he says. "I could plan on moving my production out of China but it would be very expensive and it could take me several years. I don't want to do that if things get solved. All I can do is batten down the hatches and be more conservative so that I can try and maintain the stability of my businesses. That means lower raises, less hiring, less capital expenditure, slower growth."

The Tax Foundation, a tax policy nonprofit, estimates the tariffs already in place will shrink the size of the U.S. economy by $30bn and eliminate nearly 100,000 fulltime jobs over the long run. "That's not to say there won't be a negative impact in the meantime," says Erica York, Tax Foundation analyst. "But we estimate that it will take longer for the full effects to filter through the economy to build up to the almost 100,000 job loss. As long as those tariffs stay in place, those effects will remain. And as more tariffs get added, those effects will get worse."

In theory, tariffs are supposed to protect domestic firms' market share by raising prices on foreign goods, so consumer demand shifts toward goods made at home. In practice, however, tariffs have significant downsides—they raise prices, expose the economy to trade retaliation and alienate key trade partners, says Jeffrey Kucik Assistant Professor of Political Science, University of Arizona. "Tariffs are a high-risk strategy because you're trying to use this blunt instrument to promote domestic job or wage growth," he says. "But in doing so, you're putting more jobs at risk than you're directly benefitting through the protectionist measure."

There's uncertainty with U.S. energy projects, as well, which could have ramifications for U.S. jobs and the economy. For instance, the Cactus II pipeline, which is a $1.1 billion project from Plains All American Pipeline LP to transport crude oil from the prolific Permian Basin, is now having to pay tariffs on steel that is critical to the project. While the majority of the project cost is comprised of U.S. material and labor—including over 2,500 construction jobs—the construction requires line pipe specifications produced by only three steel mills in the world—none of which exist in the U.S. Following the implementation of tariffs on steel imported from Greece, the project has been burdened with an additional $40 million in costs.

"With the U.S. natural gas and oil industry leading the energy and innovation revolution, it is of the upmost importance that the industry continues to operate without market restrictions," said Kyle Isakower, the Vice President of Regulatory and Economic Policy at American Petroleum Institute (API). "Not only does our industry support over 10 million jobs across the U.S. but American energy has reduced the trade deficit by about $250 billion over the last decade. We're poised to be a net exporter of crude oil by 2026, which will help continue to close our trade deficit and bring cleaner energy to others around the world. Unfortunately, tariffs and quotas create major uncertainty for the U.S. oil and natural gas industry, and as a result, important energy projects, and the associated jobs, could be at risk."

Consumer Confusion

While a majority of Americans (82%) are aware of recent news about the trade war and increased tariffs, less than half (46%) feel knowledgeable about them, according a survey of 1,400 Americans fielded by (E) BrandConnect, a commercial arm of The Economist Group, on behalf of API. "What does it take for Americans to fully understand the tariff impact?" asks Sage Chandler, vice president of international trade at the Consumer Technology Association. "When someone they know is directly threatened by a potential job loss."

Headlines in the media may be adding to the confusion. For example, United Steelworkers, the principal steel workers union, recently ratified an agreement that increases wages for its members by 14% over the next four years. Reports point to this as a positive, noting it increases demand for U.S. steel and stabilizes jobs. But it doesn't take into account the downstream effect for other industries, says Mr. Kucik. "We're talking about what analysts estimate to be 140,000 steel workers in the entire country against more than 10 times as many workers who are employed in an industry that consumes or relies on steel in some way," he says. "We see headlines that say steel workers' wages are going up, and on the other hand we've got six million workers whose jobs or wages are threatened in some way by the increase in steel prices."

The Impact on Various Sectors

"The balance on jobs is hard to say," says Gary Hufbauer, nonresident senior fellow and trade specialist at the Petersen Institute for International Economics. "But what's not hard to calculate is that you're reducing the productivity of the economy. All calculations show that over a period of time, the contributions of globalization of imports and exports, investments as well as trade, have been a big driver in increased productivity in the economy. From the second World War up to 2005, there was huge growth in international trade and foreign direct investment. This was a major contribution to raising living standards in the U.S., Europe and other advanced countries, but also India, China, and Latin America."

The American Chemistry Council (ACC) estimates that retaliatory tariffs on U.S. chemical and plastics exports to China put nearly 55,000 jobs at risk. "There are chemical companies that are investing billions into building manufacturing facilities in the United States," says Ed Brzytwa, director of international trade at the ACC. "But even they don't want the tariffs because they know they'll grow more without them. We have members in Texas, Pennsylvania and Louisiana who will bear a disproportionate brunt of China's retaliatory tariffs. With many US chemical manufacturers investing in the U.S. to export to China, China's retaliatory tariffs could lead to catastrophic losses in jobs, investment, and new construction."

Ms. Baughman of Trade Partnership Worldwide estimates between 100,000 and 400,000 potential net job losses if existing tariffs remain for the long term. Steve Lamar, executive vice president of the American Apparel & Footwear Association notes that their companies employ about four million Americans. A lot of people think the apparel and footwear industry no longer exists here because a lot of end stage manufacturing is done off shore, he says. "If you're a consumer and you're judging the health of our manufacturing by what's on the labels hanging in your closet you're going to get the wrong picture because 70% of the value of an imported garment is attributed to U.S. value creation: the design, expertise, quality control, compliance, branding. All of that occurs in the U.S. Yet the label can only disclose where the end-stage final production occurs."

There are benefits to moving manufacturing offshore that people seldom talk about, says Rob Limbaugh, vice president for business development at Kicker, an Oklahoma-based maker of speakers and amplifiers for cars and boats. When the business launched 45 years ago, all of its manufacturing was done in the U.S. But as the company grew, it competed on a global stage against others that had significantly lower labor costs. In the 1990s, the company moved manufacturing to China, allowing it to price its products on parity with its competitors. "Now our company and payroll are the biggest they've ever been because we are competitive," he says. "So instead of paying someone a relatively small salary to place screws into a board, we're paying a larger salary to engineers and IT professionals and sales/

marketing professionals." Paying more people a higher wage is a benefit, he notes. "The economy has shifted for the better."

However, the trade wars are making expansion planning much more difficult. Roughly 20% of its line was impacted by the tariffs. "It's virtually impossible to do any long range planning for new products," Mr. Limbaugh says. "It has been a huge opportunity cost as our management team grapples with just what do we do about all of this. Instead of working on new products and new marketing campaigns, it's been pure defense lately."

VIEWPOINT 3

> "The contemporary system of U.S. alliances and cooperative security partnerships has conferred a number of strategic advantages that make the hassle worth its attendant risks."

Alliances Bring Competitive Advantages and Also Risks

Kathleen J. McInnis

In the following viewpoint Kathleen J. McInnis argues that, although the Founding Fathers cautioned against forming alliances that could make the U.S. beholden to other nations, there have been many advantages to such partnerships throughout U.S. history. Kathleen J. McInnis is a senior fellow at the Center for Strategic and International Studies and an adjunct faculty member of Syracuse University's Maxwell School of Citizenship and Public Affairs.

As you read, consider the following questions:

1. What event is often cited as the beginning of the modern global system?
2. How did the U.S. shape the global system after World War II?
3. What is the EDI?

"The Competitive Advantages and Risks of Alliances," by Kathleen J. McInnis, The Heritage Foundation, October 30, 2019. Reprinted by permission.

Winston Churchill once famously quipped, "There is only one thing worse than fighting with allies, and that is fighting without them." So it goes for the complex web of security relationships that the United States maintains with states around the globe. Alliances and partnerships between sovereign states are often exasperatingly difficult to manage; domestic politics, burden sharing, and diverging strategic considerations create friction points that threaten to collapse them altogether.2

Despite the enormous amount of time and attention that U.S. leaders devote to maintaining alliances, allies and partners often make policy choices that are at odds with U.S. foreign and national security priorities. Further, the Founders admonished us to beware of "entangling alliances" that could embroil the United States in conflicts and conflagrations that were not necessarily in our interest.3 It is hardly surprising, therefore, that successive Administrations going back at least to 1949 have grumbled about equitable sharing of the security burden and have approached the topic of alliances overall with a note of ambivalence.

Yet since the end of World War II, successive Administrations have also determined that, despite these philosophical reservations and everyday frustrations, the contemporary system of U.S. alliances and cooperative security partnerships has conferred a number of strategic advantages that make the hassle worth its attendant risks. This "hub-and-spoke" alliance system is unique in human history; it has evolved into an unprecedented set of institutions and collaborative patterns that undergird a higher degree of global stability among sovereign states than history might otherwise have predicted.4

Militarily, the system allows the United States to advance its interests, perform expeditionary operations, and "defend in depth" at considerably lower cost than would otherwise be possible. Economically, it has allowed the United States to set the rules of international trade and finance and, on balance, remain well positioned to reap the advantages of that system. In aggregate, the system of alliances and security partnerships that the United States currently leads has afforded enormous strategic advantages to both the U.S. and those states that participate in it.

Evolution of the U.S.-Led International Security System

To understand alliances today, we need first to understand how we got here. Thucydides tells us that alliances have been an enduring feature of war and conflict for thousands of years.5 Multilateral military arrangements allow states (and their historical analogues) to aggregate their capabilities and collaborate on common security challenges.

Since the signing of the Treaty of Tordesillas between Spain and Portugal in 1494—an event that some strategic scholars point to as the beginning of the modern global system6—alliances have been formed between nation-states and their proxies in order to wage war against common adversaries. Alliances at that time were essentially agreements by European empires to combine military and economic assets in pursuit of political objectives. The European continent was the stage for many of these conflicts between states. However, colonies provided both critical resources as well as logistical bases for European capitals, and as global empires gradually expanded and grew in strategic importance, European territories around the world were drawn into supporting these alliances and were themselves made the subject of imperial competition.

The world wars during the first half of the 20th century brought the imperial system of global order crashing down. The European colonial powers no longer had the wherewithal either to maintain their global possessions or to lead the international system. As the United States became the dominant global power in the wake of those wars, it shaped the global system in a manner more consistent with its own anti-imperial values.7 It did this by building its security and strategic relationships in two primary ways: through formal strategic-political institutions such as the United Nations and the North Atlantic Treaty Organization

(NATO) and by working with newly sovereign states rather than by taking over the possession of colonial territories.

In the aftermath of World War II and as the Cold War with the Union of Soviet Socialist Republics (USSR) took shape, the U.S. and its security partners decided to integrate economic instruments into their security calculations.8 As the theory went, doing so would make states more resilient against the specter of Communism and Soviet expansionism. Hence, European reconstruction was accompanied by the Marshall Plan and NATO. NATO itself was designed with the economic and social policy compatibility of its member states in mind.

Globally, the Bretton-Woods system, including the World Bank Group and the International Monetary Fund (IMF), would help to reconstruct European economies, facilitate trade among free-market economies, and, when possible, help newly independent states transform themselves from colonial territories to full-fledged participants in the international economy.9 Security relationships with the United States, including the U.S. extended nuclear deterrence umbrella, helped to make allies in Europe and Asia capable of withstanding Soviet influence operations.10

The design of an international system that benefited a wide variety of stakeholders was not an entirely altruistic calculation by U.S. post–World War II leaders. The war and the nuclear age that followed it underscored the fact that the continental United States was no longer protected by the Atlantic and Pacific Oceans.

Looking to the experience of Europe and Asia during the war and anxious to avoid a conflict that would comparably damage the American homeland, defense planners pursued a strategy of "defense in depth."11 By positioning U.S. forces and capabilities forward in territories closer to adversaries, conflicts could be fought and won without directly affecting the continental United States. Basing agreements and alliance commitments, enabled in part by friendly economic relations and a common desire to contain the spread of Communism, were reached between the United States and a variety of countries in order to implement this defense-in-depth strategy. By the end of the Cold War, the United States had constructed a network of security relationships with sovereign states that was generally supportive of U.S. leadership of that system.

The end of the Cold War and the collapse of the Soviet threat around which the U.S. security system was organized led to a degree of soul-searching among scholars and policymakers: Why maintain these alliances and security relationships absent the threat they were designed to counter?12 These concerns proved short-lived, however, as allies and partners began to organize their security relationships and priorities around the collective management of regional crises and threats, particularly in the Middle East, Africa, and Southeastern Europe.

The United States used its existing alliance and security partnerships to adopt an expeditionary defense posture, retaining some key sites abroad that were critical for force projection (such as Ramstein Air Force Base in Germany) while closing bases and infrastructure that were no longer deemed necessary. (Such overseas bases have also been critical to managing regional "rogue" states such as Iraq, North Korea, and Iran—the latter two primarily through deterrence and forward-stationed troops and the former through active containment measures such as no-fly zones.)

The terrorist attacks of September 11, 2001, brought home the fact that there were key threats to the U.S. homeland that were not state-based: Ungoverned spaces provided the terrain for violent extremist groups to organize and metastasize into threats with a global reach. As the United States, in response, began to wage campaigns in Afghanistan, Iraq, and eventually Syria, the Department of Defense (DOD) subsequently expanded its programs to "build partner capacity" by working with fragile states in order to help them expand their capacity to govern and also, critically, their ability to eliminate threats posed by violent extremist organizations within their territory. As then-Secretary of Defense Robert Gates noted:

Building the governance and security capacity of other countries was a critical element of our strategy in the Cold War.... But it is even more urgent in a global security environment where, unlike the Cold War, the most likely and lethal threats—an American city poisoned or reduced to rubble—will likely emanate from fractured or failing states, rather than aggressor states.13

The American expeditionary military posture, including key staging and logistical sites, has remained critical to enabling U.S. counterterrorism and capacity-building operations in theaters around the world. The security networks that the United States constructed as part of this strategic shift have also helped the U.S. to achieve other transnational security objectives, including nuclear counterproliferation.

The Russian annexation of Ukraine's Crimean Peninsula in 2014, along with near-simultaneous island building by China in the South China Sea, led U.S. policymakers to conclude that these powers are willing to use military tools to advance their strategic objectives and, in the process, damage the interests of the United States and its allies and partners. This emerging "strategic competition" with other powers has added to the scope and scale of the challenges with which the U.S.-led security order— already busy managing North Korea and Iran and countering violent extremists—must grapple. As the 2017 National Security Strategy notes:

China and Russia challenge American power, influence, and interests, attempting to erode American security and prosperity. They are determined to make economies less free and less fair, to grow their militaries, and to control information and data to repress their societies and expand their influence. At the same time, the dictatorships of the Democratic People's Republic of Korea and the Islamic Republic of Iran are determined to destabilize regions, threaten Americans and our allies, and brutalize their own people. Transnational threat groups, from jihadist terrorists to transnational criminal organizations, are actively trying to harm Americans. While these challenges differ in nature and magnitude, they are fundamentally contests between those who value human dignity and freedom and those who oppress individuals and enforce uniformity.14

This has led to a hybrid of the defense in depth and expeditionary military postures. The European Deterrence Initiative (EDI), for example, is a U.S.-led effort to:

1. Continue to enhance our deterrent and defense posture throughout the theater by positioning the right capabilities in key locations in order to respond to adversarial threats in a timely manner.
2. Assure our NATO allies and partners of the United States' commitment to Article 5 and the territorial integrity of all NATO nations.
3. Increase the capability and readiness of U.S. Forces, NATO allies, and regional partners, allowing for a faster response in the event of any aggression by an adversary against the sovereign territory of NATO nations.15

Simultaneously, the U.S. has conducted counterterrorism and capacity-building operations in Afghanistan, in Iraq, and to some extent in Syria, using logistical infrastructure in Europe and the Middle East. None of this would be possible were it not for robust U.S. strategic and security relationships with allies around the world.

In summary, since the end of World War II, the United States—in contrast to the global powers that preceded America's rise—has worked to establish an international security system of sovereign states and international institutions rooted in relatively advantageous economic relationships. After the end of the Cold War, that system adapted to perform crisis management tasks. In the wake of the September 11 attacks, the system broadened still further as the United States partnered with fragile, weak, and failing states to improve the capacity of their security institutions to manage threats emanating from their territories before they could become global threats. In this network of formal and informal security relationships, the U.S. serves as the central foundation (the hub) for a global defense and military architecture (the spokes) that manages regional and international security challenges.16

Defining Alliances

Given the centrality of alliances to United States defense and security planning, as well as to grand strategy in general, it is somewhat surprising that contemporary examples of alliances remain rather poorly understood. Part of the confusion stems from the variety of ways in which scholars define the term "alliances."17 Insofar as there is consensus, it is generally held that alliances are some sort of agreements between states to render military support against an external threat under predetermined conditions.18 It is also generally understood that states make alliances in order to aggregate their military capabilities relative to external threats.

All of this makes sense to some degree: The overwhelming bulk of analyses of alliance structures, processes, formation, and so on have been derived primarily from cases involving Western European states, their empires,19 or both and often focus on historical periods up to the end of the Cold War, with comparatively little attention paid to alliances in the period following the Cold War.20

Thus, confusion surrounding the definition of "alliances," coupled with a lack of analysis of military alliances in the post–Cold War era, has limited our understanding of contemporary multilateral military alignments, contributing to an overall confusion about the utility and risks of the U.S.-led global security system. For example, up until the end of World War II, the terms "alliance" and "coalition" were interchangeable, as both referred to acts by states to prosecute military operations jointly against a common threat.21

Parsing out coalitions from alliances has not always been a terribly important distinction to make: Alliances were often formed with the specific intention of prosecuting immediate or prospective coalition warfare or to prepare for the eventuality that warfare might occur. Furthermore, alliances, particularly during the Cold War, had a sense of unanimity to them; it was unthinkable that not all NATO allies might respond to an incursion by the Warsaw Pact, vagaries in Article V notwithstanding.

This is not generally the case today. Contemporary international organizations and alliances are often formed without the specific goal of collaboratively conducting military operations, and when international organizations or other institutions do decide to undertake multilateral military operations, they often do so utilizing a subset of their membership. Not all NATO members have participated in all of NATO's post–Cold War operations.

Today, this U.S.-led hub-and-spoke system includes a variety of different strategic arrangements, most of which do not fit commonly accepted definitions of alliances. These arrangements include:

- International institutions, such as the United Nations Security Council and the Organization for Security and Cooperation in Europe (OSCE), to contend with security challenges;
- Multilateral military organizations like the North Atlantic Treaty Organization (NATO) alliance itself;
- Explicit agreements between states, such as the mutual defense pact between the United States and the Republic of Korea, to provide mutual military support in times of crisis;
- Participation by states, such as those that contributed to the International Security Assistance Force in Afghanistan, in military coalitions;
- Strategic alignments between states, such as the U.S. relationship with Israel, that are not underpinned by a treaty arrangement; and
- Bilateral, informal partnerships with other states.

It is difficult to determine the utility of these multilateral alignments without an appreciation of their various forms and how they contribute overall to U.S. and global security. In the first instance, motivations for different states' participation in this system vary, which is why these relationships range from highly formalized treaty-established agreements on the one end to informal security cooperative arrangements on the other. Some are designed to assist states as they grapple with internal security challenges. Others are focused on deterring and, if necessary, defeating an external threat.

Some states with adversarial relationships join multilateral security institutions at least in part in order to tether (and be tethered to) their adversaries, thereby (counterintuitively) advancing their own national security interests. The involvement of Greece and Turkey in NATO is one such example.[22] Some states choose to participate in multinational military coalitions in order to advance interests that have little to do with the mission or operation in question.[23] A variety of states participating in the NATO-led International Security Assistance Force in Afghanistan, for example, did so in order to affirm their solidarity with other NATO countries or their bilateral relationships with the United States.[24]

From a policymaking standpoint, understanding this wide variety of motivations is critical. Without an appreciation for why and how states join these arrangements in the first place, it is difficult to make policy judgements about the level of risk they might be willing to shoulder in the event of multilateral military operations or other activities—or, indeed, for what type of security challenges they would consider employing military force at all.

Our standard conception of alliances and their de facto focus on military aspects of statecraft are becoming dangerously outdated, in part because they are rooted in realpolitik-inspired notions of military strength and capability aggregation. While these are, of course, essential aspects of alliances, they by no means capture the sum total of the role alliances play in contemporary international relations and strategic policymaking.

As noted, more often than not, formal alliances are undergirded by close economic and political ties that serve as a key way to ensure the continued harmonization of the signatory parties' overall political and strategic views. The more formal the alliance arrangement is, the more likely it is to be complemented by a trade agreement or close economic ties, many of which arguably benefit the United States.25 While most NATO-watchers are well versed in that alliance's Article 4 (crisis planning) or Article 5 (collective defense) Treaty of Washington provisions, Article 2 has been all but forgotten:

> The Parties will contribute toward the further development of peaceful and friendly international relations by strengthening their free institutions, by bringing about a better understanding of the principles upon which these institutions are founded, and by promoting conditions of stability and well-being. They will seek to eliminate conflict in their international economic policies and will encourage economic collaboration between any or all of them.26

This logic—that economic interdependence must underpin security institutions for them to be successful in the long term—is arguably why the U.S. sought the development of trade relationships among postwar democracies.27 It is also why global economic institutions such as the World Bank and IMF were established alongside the United Nations Security Council.28 Less formal security arrangements are generally accompanied by sales of U.S. defense equipment and other matériel to partner countries; in fact, foreign military sales were at one time a gauge by which U.S. versus Soviet global influence was measured.29

This aspect of international relations does not always function perfectly (hence the trade wars with Japan in the late 20th century), but on balance, it has served to create an interdependent group of states, led by the United States, that resolve issues among each other in a peaceful manner. It has also created a series of relationships that, although challenging to manage on a day-to-day basis, are surprisingly durable in the long run. Whether this will continue to be the case in the future is a major question among strategists today.

The Contemporary Hub-and-Spoke Security System: Risks and Advantages

The alliance system that the U.S. began to construct at the end of World War II is unique in human history and has afforded the United States a number of important strategic and economic advantages. If today's world is characterized by strategic competitions with other great powers, however, as the 2017 U.S. National Security Strategy suggests, the question becomes whether the U.S. will continue to find that the advantages of the hub-and-spoke system are enough to justify its perpetuation.

The hub-and-spoke system possesses both risks and advantages to the United States that policymakers must consider as they evaluate its contemporary and future utility. The key risks include:

- **Burden-sharing.** Questions about whether allies are truly shouldering their collective security responsibilities are perennial in alliance management. In a NATO context, such questions have been raised since the founding of the alliance in 1949. Very few states today spend as much on their defense programs as the United States does, and many NATO allies struggle to meet an agreed-upon goal of 2 percent of gross domestic product (GDP) on defense.30

  Some would ask what use an alliance is if other states do not have sufficient military capabilities to advance common objectives? Others contend, however, that earlier NATO discussions of burden sharing included the moral dimensions of allied solidarity in the face of an existential expansive Communist threat. According to this view, today's debates would therefore be better characterized as debates about cost sharing rather than burden sharing. In any event, debates swirl around whether allies are paying their fair share.

- **Entanglement.** Within asymmetric alliances, most allies are fearful that the United States will either abandon them in a crisis (abandonment) or involve them in a crisis in a manner that they would not otherwise choose (entrapment). As the Founders warned, entanglement in the affairs of other states and their security challenges is a concern for the United States as well. To what extent are U.S. views of strategy and foreign policy choices influenced by allies and partners? Might we have the same perception of the Russian or Iranian threat were it not for our close allies in those regions? What are the risks of being drawn into a conflict that might prompt nuclear escalation?

- **Inappropriate Security Partnerships.** As the hub-and-spoke network of security relationships has expanded in order to prosecute counterterrorism and capacity-building strategies since September 11, 2001, questions have arisen regarding the efficacy of many of these partnerships. At the heart of the issue is whether building security forces in states with fragile governments—by, for example, providing training, equipment, and institutional support—might actually make the United States less secure in the long term.

For one thing, partners on the ground may have short-term and long-term interests that are very different from those of the United States and may use their enhanced military capabilities to go beyond the objectives for which the assistance was intended. U.S. security assistance to Mali led to the provision of professional military education and training. A separatist rebellion launched in late 2011 by members of the minority ethnic Tuareg community aggravated intramilitary and political tensions in the country, leading to a military coup by junior officers

in March 2012 that was spearheaded by Captain Amadou Sonogo, who had been a recipient of that training,31
- **Strategic Insolvency.** Some observers of U.S. defense policy are increasingly concerned that the gap between America's defense spending and its global responsibilities is widening. According to this view, budget unpredictability exacerbated by the 2011 Budget Control Act ("sequestration"), along with readiness issues, nearly two decades of war, personnel retention, and other factors, has left the DOD ill prepared to meet its own goals as articulated in the 2018 National Defense Strategy. Elements of this argument can be found in theories of imperial overstretch;32 the National Defense Strategy Commission (NDSC) calls it a possibility of "strategic insolvency."33 Within the foreseeable future, the U.S. may no longer have the capabilities to defend its allies in more than one theater without significantly reinvesting in its defense program, significantly scaling back its level of ambition, or both.34

The principal advantages of the hub-and-spoke system include:

- **Global Reach.** One of the key reasons for building the U.S.-led defense architecture in the first place was to be able to fight the nation's wars far away from the American homeland. This rationale still holds. The United States would not have been able to plan and execute operations around the world like its move into Afghanistan, which occurred within a month after the September 11 terrorist attacks, were it not for its network of military bases and access agreements in the U.S. European Command and U.S. Central Command areas of responsibility.35
- **Lower Costs.** Despite the considerable amount of political hay being made from burden-sharing issues, the financial costs that the U.S. would have to shoulder to accomplish its strategic objectives absent its hub-and-spoke system would likely be significantly higher. Allies often facilitate

the presence of U.S. forces stationed on their soil through in-kind payments. South Korea, for example, contributed the lion's share of the costs associated with building Camp Humphreys ($9.7 billion of a $10.8 billion project) and annually pays approximately 50 percent of the nonpersonnel costs for the stationing of U.S. troops.36 Further, historically speaking, imperial predecessors appear to have spent a considerably larger share of their annual budgets on the maintenance of their global military posture.

While not a perfect comparison, it is still worth observing that by some estimates, the United Kingdom spent upwards of 37 percent of its annual governmental budget on its military between 1860 and 1914.37 During the same period, the majority of Western European countries, Russia, the U.S., and Japan spent, on average, 32 percent of their annual governmental budgets on their militaries.38 In other words, "[t]axes collected by the British government were used basically to defray military expenditure and to pay interest on a national debt which had accumulated as a consequence of past wars fought to acquire and defend the empire."39 By comparison, the U.S. spent 14.75 percent of its annual budget (both mandatory and discretionary) on the defense program in 2017.40

- **Exercises and Interoperability.** The hub-and-spoke system has created a wide variety of opportunities for U.S. servicemembers to engage with their foreign counterparts to advance strategic, operational, and tactical interests collectively and ensure that servicemembers from different countries can fight together effectively. NATO, for example, has the International Military Staff (IMS) and a series of standardization agreements and exercises that help to improve interoperability among member states and partners. These preparations during peacetime help to build meaningful capabilities that can be drawn upon during crises and conflict.

- Even though Operation Iraqi Freedom was an ad-hoc coalition, for example, most experts agree that it would not have been possible to operate coherently were it not for NATO's decades of efforts to improve interoperability among its members, many of which participated in that coalition. Also, many multilateral military exercises occur outside of U.S. territories, which has the additional advantage of giving U.S. servicemembers key opportunities to understand the contours of a theater or battlespace before conflict occurs, which in turn enables better planning and preparation for an outbreak of hostilities.
- **Coalition Participants.** Another proven benefit of the hub-and-spoke system has been the willingness of other states to contribute troops, financial resources, or both to U.S.-led military coalitions. At the height of the Afghanistan campaign, 50 nations contributed troops to the International Security Assistance Force.41 Similarly, allies and partners have contributed to U.S.-led wars and operations in Korea, Vietnam, the Persian Gulf, Somalia, the Balkans, Libya, Iraq, and Syria. In addition to defraying the costs in terms of both blood and treasure that are associated with prosecuting these missions, these contributions have also served to underscore their international legitimacy.42

Given this balance sheet of risks and advantages, successive U.S. Administrations have determined that reinvesting in this hub-and-spoke system continues to benefit American interests. The amount of time and attention that day-to-day management of this system entails—on any given day, dozens of tactical-level and strategic-level issues between sovereign states must be juggled based on shifting notions of security and defense that change over time along with strategic circumstances—might suggest to a casual observer that these relationships are fragile, but the historical track record suggests the opposite. The dissolution of the Soviet Union actually led to an expansion of the hub-and-spoke system and has enabled the United States to prosecute expeditionary operations alongside a wide variety of coalition partners.

Looking to the future, however, there are reasons for concern. The U.S.'s key competitors have studied America's defense strategy or approach to waging war and appear to have concluded that fighting the United States conventionally is a losing proposition. Instead, Russia and China appear to be using a combination of military and nonmilitary tools (such as, for example, Moscow's seizure of the Crimean Peninsula and Beijing's assertion of a claim to the nine-dash line territories in the South China Sea) to achieve their objectives.

Another key tactic that these adversaries appear to be using is an attempt to disrupt the U.S.-led hub-and-spoke security network. Due to China's coercive economic policies, combined with its military reforms and expeditionary presence, some of America's allies such as Australia are facing a stark strategic choice: whether to invest in a relationship with China or with the United States.43 Others, such as Italy, have determined that no apparent conflict exists between embracing Chinese Belt and Road investments and observing their obligations to the European Union (EU) and NATO.44 Likewise, Russia's disinformation operations appear to be designed, among other things, to sow doubt in European capitals as to the utility of the institutions that the U.S. has helped to create since World War II, including NATO and the EU.45

Complicating matters, Moscow and Beijing appear to be collaborating to achieve their shared objective of displacing the United States as the center of the hub-and-spoke system. As the 2019 Worldwide Threat Assessment released by the Director of National Intelligence notes, "Russia and China seek to shape the international system and regional security dynamics and exert influence over the politics and economies of states in all regions of the world and especially in their respective backyards."46

Their apparent objective in doing so is to advance an authoritarian vision of governance and world order.47 This stands in stark contrast to the international order that the United States has fought hard to achieve over the past 70 years and that, on balance, takes human freedom and individual liberty as a starting point for political organization. From this perspective, the strategic stakes could hardly be higher.

Conclusion

Both nature and power abhor a vacuum, and both Beijing and Moscow appear to be happy to fill any space created by a U.S. retrenchment—perceived or actual—from the hub-and-spoke system. The United States therefore appears to be at a crossroads. It can either continue to view its complex network of security relationships through a transactional, cost-sharing lens, or it can instead reconsider the broader strategic value of the hub-and-spoke network as the key mechanism through which Washington can counter its great-power competitors.

Indeed, allies contribute to the U.S. and the furtherance of its interests in any number of ways, and their contributions go beyond mere dollars and cents. Regional access, prepositioning of forces and supplies, political-strategic relationships, and interoperable forces together create a "warm start" in the event of a crisis. Further, the U.S. gains intelligence and situational awareness from its global security relationships that it would not otherwise have.

Perhaps most important, however, by reinvesting in its global web of security relationships, the U.S. simultaneously is sending a message to its competitors that they will not be able to pursue their own arguably coercive agendas unchallenged. Should the U.S. let the hub-and-spoke system languish, the costs of acting alone—in diplomatic, military, and economic terms—are likely to be prohibitive. Compounding the problem, adversaries would likely take advantage of an erosion of U.S. security relations to strengthen their positions at America's expense.

Despite the hub-and-spoke network's advantages, just as questions about the appropriate U.S. role in the world remain up in the air, so too does the question of retrenchment from this system versus reinvigoration of it also remain unsettled. At least for now, however, the hub-and-spoke system will undoubtedly remain a foundational element of American strategy—if we choose to keep it.

Endnotes

1. Any views expressed in this article are strictly those of the author and do not represent the views of any organization with which she is affiliated.
2. Dwight D. Eisenhower, Crusade in Europe (New York: Doubleday, 1948), p. 4, as quoted in Robert H. Scales, Jr., "Trust, Not Technology, Sustains Coalitions," Parameters, Vol. 28, No. 4 (Winter 1998–99), https://ssi.armywarcollege.edu/pubs/parameters/articles/98winter/scales1.htm (accessed July 13, 2019).
3. David Fromkin, "Entangling Alliances," Foreign Affairs, Vol. 48, No. 4 (July 1970), pp. 688–700, https://www.foreignaffairs.com/articles/1970-07-01/entangling-alliances (accessed July 13, 2019).
4. "Hub-and-spoke" is often used to describe the U.S. system of bilateral alliances in Asia, while NATO is referred to as a "multilateral" system. These terms generally refer to formal alliance relationships; as this essay considers the totality of U.S. global security arrangements and how they have evolved over time, "hub-and-spoke" is an appropriate metaphor to describe this complex network of security relationships that has the United States at its center.
5. Thucydides, The History of the Peloponnesian War, trans. Richard Crawley (London: J.M. Dent, 1910).
6. George Modelski, "The Long Cycle of Global Politics and the Nation State," Comparative Studies in Society and History, Vol. 20, No. 2 (April 1978), pp. 214–235.
7. Kori Schake, Safe Passage: The Transition from British to American Hegemony (Cambridge, MA: Harvard University Press, 2017), esp. Chapter One. The United States has, of course, been imperfect in its application of these values and principles; the U.S. annexed Hawaii, for example.
8. "It is imperative that [there be] a much more rapid and concerted build-up of the actual strength of both the United States and the other nations of the free world. ¶ The execution of such a build-up, however, requires that the United States have an affirmative program beyond the solely defensive one of countering the threat posed by the Soviet Union. This program must light the path to peace and order among nations in a system based on freedom and justice.… Further, it must envisage the political and economic measures with which and the military shield behind which the free world can work to frustrate the Kremlin design by the strategy of the cold war.… The only sure victory lies in the frustration of the Kremlin design by the steady development of the moral and material strength of

the free world and its projection into the Soviet world in such a way as to bring about an internal change in the Soviet system…. ¶ In summary, we must, by means of a rapid and sustained build-up of the political, economic and military strength of the free world, and by means of an affirmative program intended to wrest the initiative from the Soviet Union, confront it with convincing evidence of the determination and ability of the free world to frustrate the Kremlin design of a world dominated by its will….'' Conclusions and Recommendations" in NSC 68: United States Objectives and Programs for National Security (April 14, 1950): A Report to the President Pursuant to the President's Directive of January 31, 1950, National Security Council, April 7, 1950, https://fas.org/irp/offdocs/nsc-hst/nsc-68.htm (accessed July 15, 2019).
9. World Bank, "History," http://www.worldbank.org/en/about/archives/history (accessed July 15, 2019), and International Monetary Fund, "History: Cooperation and Reconstruction (1944–71), https://www.imf.org/external/about/histcoop.htm (accessed July 15, 2019).
10. NSC 68: United States Objectives and Programs for National Security, p. 68.
11. Stacie L. Pettyjohn, U.S. Global Defense Posture, 1783–2011 (Santa Monica, CA: RAND Corporation, 2012), pp. 49–96, https://www.rand.org/content/dam/rand/pubs/monographs/2012/RAND_MG1244.pdf (accessed July 15, 2019). Prepared for the U.S. Air Force by RAND Project Air Force.
12. Wallace J. Thies, Why NATO Endures (New York: Cambridge University Press, 2009).
13. U.S. Department of Defense, "Remarks as Delivered by Secretary of Defense Robert M. Gates, The Nixon Center, Washington, D.C., Wednesday, February 24, 2010," http://archive.defense.gov/speeches/speech.aspx?speechid=1425 (accessed June 17, 2019).
14. National Security Strategy of the United States of America, The White House, December 2017, pp. 2–3, https://www.whitehouse.gov/wp-content/uploads/2017/12/NSS-Final-12-18-2017-0905.pdf (accessed July 15, 2019).
15. U.S. Department of Defense, Office of the Undersecretary of Defense (Comptroller), Department of Defense Budget Fiscal Year (FY) 2020: European Deterrence Initiative, March 2019, p. 1, https://comptroller.defense.gov/Portals/45/Documents/defbudget/fy2020/fy2020_EDI_JBook.pdf (accessed June 17, 2019).
16. See note 4, supra.
17. Compounding the confusion, different scholars have sought to categorize them in different, often overlapping ways. Bruce Russett captures this ambiguity well when he lays out how different scholars—Hans Morgenthau and Kalevi J. Holsti—approach the topic of alliances. He explains that Morgenthau categorizes alliances according to whether they are (1) mutual or unilateral; (2) temporary or permanent; (3) operative or inoperative, depending on their ability to coordinate members' policies; (4) general or limited in their distribution of benefits; and (5) complementary, identical, or ideological in their scope of interest. Holsti, by contrast, organizes alliances along the following lines: (1) the situation in which commitments are to become operational, (2) the type of commitments undertaken, (3) the degree of military cooperation or integration, and (4) the geographic scope of the treaty. Bruce M. Russett, "An Empirical Typology of International Military Alliances," Midwest Journal of Political Science, Vol. 15, No. 2 (May 1971), p. 264.
18. Stephen M. Walt, The Origin of Alliances (Ithaca, NY: Cornell University Press, 1987), pp. 12–13, and Glenn H. Snyder, Alliance Politics (Ithaca, NY: Cornell

University Press, 2007), p. 4. In Walt's conception, they can be formal or informal; in Snyder's, they are formal arrangements.
19. The major exception to this is Walt's The Origin of Alliances, which looks at alliance formation in the Middle East from 1955–1979.
20. There is, of course, an enormous body of post–Cold War work exploring the particular policy and strategic dimensions of key alliance relationships, such as NATO or U.S. bilateral defense relationships in Asia. Yet the insights and assumptions regarding the formation and maintenance of those alliances are often informed by studies of alliances that predate the end of the Cold War (or, in the case of constructivism, very shortly thereafter).
21. Brett Ashley Leeds, Jeffrey M. Ritter, Sara McLaughlin Mitchell, and Andrew G. Long, "Alliance Treaty Obligations and Provisions, 1815–1944," International Interactions, Vol. 28, No. 3 (July 2002), pp. 237–260, (accessed July 15, 2019).
22. Patricia Weitsman, Dangerous Alliances: Proponents of Peace, Weapons of War (Stanford: Stanford University Press, 2004).
23. Kathleen J. McInnis, How and Why States Defect from Contemporary Military Coalitions (New York: Palgrave Macmillan, 2019).
24. Ibid.
25. Glenn Snyder refers to this as the "political penumbra" of alliances. Further, a RAND study notes, "In our analysis of aggregate U.S. bilateral trade, we find solid evidence that U.S. security commitments have significantly positive effects on U.S. bilateral trade. For example…a doubling of U.S. personnel commitments overseas could increase U.S. bilateral trade by as much as 15 percent, depending on the service, while a doubling of treaties could expand U.S. bilateral trade by 34 percent overall." Daniel Engel, Adam R. Grissom, John P. Godges, Jennifer Kavanagh, and Howard J. Schatz, Estimating the Value of Overseas Security Commitments (Santa Monica, CA: RAND Corporation, 2016), p. x, https://www.rand.org/content/dam/rand/pubs/research_reports/RR500/RR518/RAND_RR518.pdf (accessed July 15, 2019).
26. North Atlantic Treaty, Article 2, April 4, 1949, last updated April 10, 2019, https://www.nato.int/cps/en/natolive/official_texts_17120.htm (accessed July 15, 2019). Emphasis added.
27. G. John Ikenberry, After Victory: Institutions, Strategic Restraint, and the Rebuilding of Order After Major Wars (Princeton, NJ: Princeton University Press, 2001) pp. 162–214.
28. Ibid. See also I. M. Destler, "America's Uneasy Relationship with Free Trade," Harvard Business Review, April 28, 2016, https://hbr.org/2016/04/americas-uneasy-history-with-free-trade (accessed June 18, 2019).
29. Robert E. Harkavy, Bases Abroad: The Global Foreign Military Presence (Stockholm: Stockholm International Peace Research Institute, 1989), p. 5.
30. Press release, "Wales Summit Declaration Issued by the Heads of State and Government Participating in the Meeting of the North Atlantic Council in Wales," North Atlantic Treaty Organization, September 5, 2014, https://www.nato.int/cps/en/natohq/official_texts_112964.htm#def-exp (accessed June 18, 2019).
31. Martin Vogl, "Mali Coup Leaders Partially Reopen Airport," Associated Press, March 26, 2012, http://archive.boston.com/news/world/africa/articles/2012/03/26/mali_protesters_seek_return_to_order_after_coup/ (accessed July 15, 2019), and Simon J. Powelson, Enduring Engagement Yes, Episodic Engagement No: Lessons for SOF from Mali, Thesis, Naval

32. Paul Kennedy, The Rise and Fall of the Great Powers (New York: Random House, 1987).
33. National Defense Strategy Commission, Providing for the Common Defense: The Assessment and Recommendations of the National Defense Strategy Commission, released November 14, 2018, p. xii, https://www.usip.org/sites/default/files/2018-11/providing-for-the-common-defense.pdf (accessed July 15, 2019).
34. Rick Berger and Mackenzie Eaglen, "'Hard Choices' and Strategic Insolvency: Where the National Defense Strategy Falls Short," War on the Rocks, May 16, 2019. https://warontherocks.com/2019/05/hard-choices-and-strategic-insolvency-where-the-national-defense-strategy-falls-short/ (accessed July 15, 2019).
35. Council on Foreign Relations, "The U.S. War in Afghanistan: 1999–2019," CFR Timeline, https://www.cfr.org/timeline/us-war-afghanistan (accessed July 15, 2019).
36. Mark E. Manyin, Emma Chanlett-Avery, and Brock R. Williams, "South Korea: Background and U.S. Relations," Congressional Research Service In Focus No. 10165, updated May 20, 2019, https://fas.org/sgp/crs/row/IF10165.pdf (accessed June 18, 2019), and Christine Kim, "US Forces Chief Says South Korea Paid for 90 Percent of Biggest Overseas Base," Reuters, June 28, 2018, https://www.reuters.com/article/us-usa-southkorea-base/u-s-forces-chief-says-south-korea-paid-for-90-percent-of-biggest-overseas-base-idUSKBN1JP09X (accessed June 18, 2019).
37. Patrick K. O'Brien, "The Costs and Benefits of British Imperialism 1846–1914," Past & Present, Vol. 120, No. 1 (August 1988), p. 187.
38. Ibid.
39. Ibid.
40. Congressional Budget Office, "The Federal Budget in 2017: An Infographic," March 2018, https://www.cbo.gov/publication/53624 (accessed July 13, 2019). Figure derived from calculating the amount of defense spending in 2017 ($590 billion) as a percentage of an overall federal budget of $4 trillion.
41. North Atlantic Treaty Organization, International Security Assistance Force, "International Security Assistance Force (ISAF): Key Facts and Figures," October 8, 2012, https://www.nato.int/isaf/placemats_archive/2012-10-08-ISAF-Placemat.pdf (accessed June 18, 2019).
42. Olivier Schmitt refers to this as "legitimacy aggregation." Olivier Schmitt, Allies that Count: Junior Partners in Coalition Warfare (Washington: Georgetown University Press, 2011).
43. Neil Irwin, "Australia and the U.S. Are Old Allies. China's Rise Changes the Equation," The New York Times, May 11, 2019, https://www.nytimes.com/2019/05/11/upshot/australia-relationship-china-us-trade.html (accessed July 15, 2019).
44. Andrew Chatzky, "China's Belt and Road Gets a Win in Italy," Council on Foreign Relations, March 27, 2019, https://www.cfr.org/article/chinas-belt-and-road-gets-win-italy (accessed July 15, 2019).
45. Daniel R. Coats, Director of National Intelligence, "Worldwide Threat Assessment of the US Intelligence Community," statement before the Select Committee on Intelligence, U.S. Senate, January 29, 2019, pp. 5–6, https://www.dni.gov/files/

ODNI/documents/2019-ATA-SFR---SSCI.pdf (accessed July 15, 2019). See also Todd C. Helmus, Elizabeth Bodine-Baron, Andrew Radin, Madeline Magnuson, Joshua Mendelsohn, William Marcellino, Andriy Bega, and Zev Winkelman, Russian Social Media Influence: Understanding Russian Propaganda in Eastern Europe (Santa Monica, CA: RAND Corporation, 2018), https://www.rand.org/content/dam/rand/pubs/research_reports/RR2200/RR2237/RAND_RR2237.pdf (accessed July 15, 2019).

46. Coats, "Worldwide Threat Assessment of the US Intelligence Community," p. 4.
47. Ibid., pp. 4 and 25.

VIEWPOINT 4

> *"Suppose we knew that a trade reform positively affected a country's growth rate. What would that look like, empirically? Could we verify and measure the effect?"*

Trade Reform Leads to Economic Growth
Brian C. Albrecht

In this viewpoint, Brian C. Albrecht tackles the question of how free trade polices correspond to indications of economic growth. He wants to use these figures to tease out an answer to the question of whether or not trade is really good for economic growth or not. Brian Albrecht puts together some of these numbers and weaves them together to lay out his argument. Brian C. Albrecht is a researcher from the American Institute for Economic Research, a think tank based in Massachusetts that is funded through investments in companies like Chevron and ExxonMobil, as well as industrialists like Charles Koch.

As you read, consider the following questions:

1. How has trade policy changed over time according to the viewpoint?
2. Did the trade reforms discussed in the viewpoint ultimately lead to growth?

"Freer Trade and Economic Growth: Evidence of the Relationship," by Brian C. Albrecht, American Institute for Economic Research, July 3, 2019. https://www.aier.org/article/freer-trade-and-economic-growth-evidence-of-the-relationship/. Licensed under CC BY-4.0 International.

3. Is this viewpoint's perspective ultimately for or against free trade policies?

Economists agree that trade is good for economic growth, right? While our economic understanding of the benefits of trade goes back to the very origins of the field, strong empirical estimates of trade's effect on growth have been harder to establish. Some countries that liberalized trade experienced massive growth; others floundered.

Overall, it has proven a tricky empirical question.

In an influential 1992 article published in the Journal of Economic Perspectives, Dani Rodrik argued that "in most of the countries that have undertaken radical trade reforms in the 1980s, the direct efficiency consequences of trade liberalization are still uncertain and likely to be small." In a follow-up survey conducted by Rodrik and Francesco Rodríguez in 2000, the authors concluded that "the relationship between trade policy and economic growth remains very much an open question" and "is far from having been settled on empirical grounds."

What have we learned in the 20 years since Rodríguez and Rodrik's article? A new NBER working paper by Douglas Irwin summarizes recent work estimating the relationship between trade reform and economic growth.

First, Irwin shows just how much trade policy has been reformed over time. With more evidence at hand, Irwin points out that estimates from cross-country regressions often put the effect at a one to two percentage-point increase in growth from trade liberalization. Notice that this is an increase in the growth rate, not an increase in output. A one percentage-point increase is huge. Incomes growing at 3 percent double in roughly 23 years, quadruple in 46 years. Incomes growing at 4 percent double in 18 years, quadruple in 35 years. Small differences in growth rates result in huge differences in income over time.

Other studies have looked at particular industries in particular countries in more detail; the results also show a positive impact of opening to trade. As Irwin puts it, "A consistent finding is that trade reforms have a positive impact on economic growth, on average, but as one would expect the effects differ considerably across countries."

One of the reasons that economists in 2019 have a better understanding of the effects of trade reforms is that the major trade liberalizations have had more time to take effect. "The great trade reform wave of the late 1980s and early 1990s," Irwin writes, "provides new historical evidence on the matter. There is no one perfect method that can provide decisive evidence on this question, so researchers have tried to understand the relationship using a variety of approaches." And that reform wave provides a lot of data points.

Trade reforms often involved multiple policies, carried out in multiple steps, where countries went about "devaluing their currencies and unifying their exchange rates, allowing exporters to retain foreign currency earnings, reducing licensing and quantitative restrictions, and then—often last in the mix—cutting tariffs, usually on intermediate goods first and consumer goods later, sometimes much later."

When those tariffs finally were cut, they were cut immensely. Tariff rates in developing countries drop from a high of more than 35 percent in the early 1980s to below 10 percent by 2010. Similarly, Martin and Ng (2004) calculate the weighted-average tariff in developing countries and find that it declined by similar amounts. Of interest for policy discussions about the political feasibility of lowering trade barriers, Martin and Ng find that three-quarters of the tariff reduction came from unilateral actions taken by the countries involved.

However, this liberalization over time was not consistent across the globe. South Asian countries, such as India, Bangladesh, and Sri Lanka, saw the largest decline in tariffs, whereas Africa and the Middle East did not change their policies much.

Did these reforms actually lead to growth? It is difficult to conclude definitively. As Irwin puts it, "Standard theory suggests that reducing trade barriers should lead to efficiency gains. But why might it be expected to increase economic growth as well? … When policy reforms (trade related or otherwise) are limited and phased in, there is no reason to expect an immediate burst of growth."

Suppose we knew that a trade reform positively affected a country's growth rate. What would that look like, empirically? Could we verify and measure the effect? It is extremely difficult to isolate an individual factor in economic growth since economists do not run country-wide experiments. Instead, economists must compile varied evidence to come to tentative conclusions.

The first (and most common) type of evidence is cross-country regressions. Irwin cites a recent World Bank Economic Review paper by Romain Wacziarg and Karen Welch. The authors find that "trade reform had a positive, economically large, and statistically significant impact on growth and investment" of around one percentage-point.

But, on further reflection, lumping all trade reforms together and considering the effect is a bit odd. Not all tariffs are equal. And reducing some tariffs might have a bigger effect on growth than others. A final-goods tariff might not matter much, for example, while a tariff on investment may have a large impact on growth over time. If that is the case, we should expect reducing investment tariffs to have a larger impact. In a 2013 paper, Estevadeordal and Taylor find that a 25 percent reduction in tariffs on capital goods is associated with a roughly 1 percentage-point increase in economic growth, compared to non-liberalizers.

In order to move from "associated with" to "caused by," Irwin looks at studies using synthetic controls. In a synthetic-control study, the econometrician attempts to construct a "synthetic" country against which one can judge the performance of an actual country. The synthetic control represents the best guess of what would have happened if the reforming country had not reformed. It is an attempt to create a counterfactual in order to make more-relevant comparisons. Of course, making a causal argument still

A War over the Panama Trade Agreement

Since taking office, President Obama hasn't exactly been a beacon for trade liberalization and open markets. Instead, he has pandered to his protectionist, no faith in America's competitive advantage allies in Congress, allowing them to pass legislation that sparked a trade war with Mexico, our third largest trading partner, and could reduce imports of steel and other manufactured goods.

However, there could be some positive news for supporters of free trade as the Administration has signaled it may send the Panama Free Trade Agreement to Congress for approval. Panama could be the starting off point for passage of the other pending agreements currently being held up, Colombia and South Korea.

Below are just a few reasons why the Panama FTA should be approved without delay:

- Levels the playing field by removing trade and investment barriers that have hindered American exports to Panama. While more than ninety percent of imports from Panama are duty free, U.S. products still face tariffs when entering Panama. The Panama FTA will eliminate this trade barrier and open new markets for U.S. product
- Opens up $5.25 billion in contracts American firms will be allowed to compete for when Panama begins the expansion of the Panama Canal.
- Lowers taxes for Americans and Panamanians. A tariff is nothing more than a tax on international commerce. Since tariffs and trade barriers amount to government-imposed costs on both companies and consumers, eliminating these barriers in a free trade agreement amounts to a significant tax cut for both countries.

And maybe Panama could export a little tax reform to the U.S. Say simplifying the tax code ala President-elect, Ricardo Martinelli?

"Free the Panama Trade Agreement", by Kelsey Zahourek, **Americans for Tax Reform**, May 5, 2009.

requires a host of assumptions. Nevertheless, synthetic controls provide another form of evidence, and that evidence indicates that reforms improve economic growth.

The biggest change for researchers considering the effects of trade on growth over the past 20 years has been the greater availability of data. Economists now have firm-level data in developing countries that help determine what economic adjustments were made after reforms. For example, Amiti and Konings (2007) use plant-level data on imported inputs from Indonesia from 1991 to 2001. They estimate that a 10 percentage-point reduction in input tariffs led to a 12 percent productivity gain for importing firms. For output tariffs, a 10 percentage-point reduction was associated with a productivity gain of 1–6 percent. Irwin cites other papers with similar results.

While we know a lot more than we knew 20 years ago, questions remain about how much of the increase in growth can be attributed to trade reform and how much should be attributed to other market reforms made at the same time. Even if the reduction of trade barriers accounts for only a small part of the observed increase in growth, however, the cumulative gains from reform appear to be substantial. Irwin concludes by quoting Estevadeordal and Taylor: "Is there any other single policy prescription of the past twenty years that can be argued to have contributed between 15 percent and 20 percent to developing country income?" I highly doubt it.

VIEWPOINT 5

> "The root of the problem is the way international corporate income is taxed. The current system is based on an approach devised almost a century ago, when large multinationals as we know them today did not exist."

Multinationals Continue to Avoid Paying Hundreds of Billions of Dollars in Tax

Miroslav Palanský

In this viewpoint, Miroslav Palanský takes a hard look at how corporations use the global economy to conceal their income from tax authorities. The situation, he says, costs countries billions of dollars in potential revenue every year. He argues that it is the result of an international finance system which has yet to adapt to a globalized world. Instead, too many monetary systems become easy to operate around, even by some of the largest companies in the world. Miroslav Palanský is a researcher at the Institute of Economic Studies, a nonprofit group based in Paris.

"How Multinationals Continue to Avoid Paying Hundreds of Billions of Dollars in Tax—New Research," by Miroslav Palanský, The Conversation, October 3, 2019. https://theconversation.com/how-multinationals-continue-to-avoid-paying-hundreds-of-billions-of-dollars-in-tax-new-research-124323. Licensed under CC BY-4.0 International.

As you read, consider the following questions:

1. How much money in corporate profits is regularly shifted around the world, according to the study cited by the author?
2. Proportionally speaking, do lower income countries lose more or less of their tax revenue through the shifting of tax revenue?
3. What are some of the ways the viewpoint suggests that the shifting around of taxable revenue can be stymied?

Tax havens have become a defining feature of the global financial system. Multinational companies can use various schemes to avoid paying taxes in countries where they make vast revenues. In new research, my colleague Petr Janský and I estimate that around US$420 billion in corporate profits is shifted out of 79 countries every year.

This equates to about US$125 billion in lost tax revenue for these countries. As a result, their state services are either underfunded or must be funded by other, often lower-income taxpayers. It contributes to rising inequality both within countries and across the world.

Given the nature of the issue, it is intrinsically difficult to detect tax avoidance or evasion. To get round this, we use data on foreign direct investment (FDI) collected by the International Monetary Fund to examine whether companies owned from tax havens report lower profits in high-tax countries compared to other companies.

We found that countries with a higher share of FDI from tax havens report profits that are systematically and significantly lower, suggesting these profits have been shifted to tax havens before being reported in high-tax countries. The strength of this relationship enables us to estimate how much more profit would be reported in each country if companies owned from tax havens reported similar profits to other companies.

We found that lower-income countries on average lose at least as much as developed countries (relative to the size of their economies). At the same time, they are less able to implement effective tools to reduce the amount of profit shifted out of their countries.

Three Channels of Profit Shifting

There are three main channels that multinationals can use to shift profits out of high-tax countries: debt shifting, registering intangible assets such as copyright or trademarks in tax havens, and a technique known as "strategic transfer pricing."

To see how these channels work, imagine that a multinational is composed of two companies, one located in a high-tax jurisdiction like Australia (company A) and one located in a low-tax jurisdiction like Bermuda (company B). Company B is a holding company and fully owns company A.

While both companies should pay tax on the profit they make in their respective countries, one of the three channels is used to shift profits from the high-tax country (Australia in our case, with a corporate income tax rate of 30%) to the low-tax country (Bermuda, with a corporate income tax rate of 0%). For every dollar shifted in this way, the multinational avoids paying 30 cents of tax.

Debt-shifting is when company A borrows money (although it does not need to) from company B and pays interest on this loan to company B. The interest payments are a cost to company A and are tax-deductible in Australia. So they effectively reduce the profit that company A reports in Australia, while increasing the profit reported in Bermuda.

In the second channel, the multinational transfers its intangible assets (such as trademarks or copyright) to company B, and company A then pays royalties to company B to use these assets. Royalties are a cost to company A and artificially lower its profit, increasing the less-taxed profit of company B.

Strategic transfer pricing, the third channel, can be used when company A trades with company B. To set prices for their trade, most countries currently use what's called the "arm's length principle." This means that prices should be set the same as they would be if two non-associated entities traded with each other.

But, in practice, it is often difficult to determine the arm's length price and there is considerable space for multinationals to set the price in a way that minimises their overall tax liabilities. Imagine company A manufactures jeans and sells them to company B, which then sells them in shops. If the cost of manufacturing a pair of jeans is US$80 and company A would be willing to sell them to unrelated company C for US$100, they would make US$20 in profit and pay US$6 in tax (at 30%) in Australia.

But if company A sells the jeans to its subsidiary company B for just US$81, it only makes US$1 in profit and so pays US$0.3 in tax in Australia. Company B then sells the jeans to unrelated company C for US$100, making US$19 in profit, but not paying any tax, since there is no corporate income tax in Bermuda. Using this scheme, the multinational evades paying US$5.7 in tax in Australia for every pair of jeans sold.

How to Stop It

The root of the problem is the way international corporate income is taxed. The current system is based on an approach devised almost a century ago, when large multinationals as we know them today did not exist. Today, individual entities that make up a multinational run separate accounts as if they were independent companies. But the multinational optimises its tax liabilities as a whole.

Instead, we should switch to what's called a unitary model of taxation. The idea is to tax the profit where the economic activity which generates it actually takes place—not where profits are reported. The multinational would report on its overall global profit and also on its activity in each country in which it operates. The governments of these countries would then be allowed to tax the multinational according to the activity in their country.

In practice, defining what exactly constitutes "economic activity which generates profit" is the tricky bit. For a multinational that manufactures phones, for example, it is not clear what part of its profit is generated by, say, the managers in California, designers in Texas, programmers in Munich, an assembly factory in China, a Singapore-based logistics company that ships the phone to Paris, the retail store in Paris that sells the phone, or the French consumer.

Different proposals for unitary taxation schemes define this tax base in various ways. The five factors most often taken into account are: location of headquarters, sales, payroll, employee headcount and assets. Different proposals give different weight to these factors.

Ultimately, introducing unitary taxation would require a global consensus on the formula used to apportion profits. And, admittedly, this would be difficult to do. As the OECD says: "It present[s] enormous political and administrative complexity and require[s] a level of international cooperation that is unrealistic to expect in the field of international taxation."

But, seeing as the current system costs governments around the world around US$125 billion annually, is global cooperation really more expensive than that?

Periodical and Internet Sources Bibliography

The following articles have been selected to supplement the diverse views presented in this chapter.

Marc Bayard, "US trade policy has failed Black and Latino workers," CNN, March 1, 2021, https://www.cnn.com/2021/03/01/perspectives/trade-policy-black-latino-workers/index.html.

Keith Bradsher, "China Is Set to Take a Hard Line on Trump's Trade Demands," *New York Times*, April 30, 2018, https://www.nytimes.com/2018/04/30/business/china-trump-trade-talks.html.

John Cassidy, "What Is Donald Trump's Trade Policy? Nobody Knows," *New Yorker*, May 1, 2018, https://www.newyorker.com/news/our-columnists/what-is-donald-trumps-trade-policy-nobody-knows.

David Frum, "This Is No Time for Protectionism," *Atlantic*, March 2, 2022, https://www.theatlantic.com/ideas/archive/2022/03/biden-economic-nationalism-state-of-the-union/623325.

Frida Ghitis, "America-first trade policy is crushing the global economy," CNN, September 1, 2019, https://www.cnn.com/2019/09/01/perspectives/trade-protectionism-us-trump/index.html.

Yuka Hayashi, "Biden's Worker-First Trade Policy Rankles Foreign Partners," *Wall Street Journal*, December 28, 2021, https://www.wsj.com/articles/bidens-worker-first-trade-policy-rankles-foreign-partners-11640716598.

Alex Kotlowitz, "The Small-Town Cost of Donald Trump's Trade Wars," *New Yorker*, December 20, 2018, https://www.newyorker.com/news/dispatch/the-small-town-cost-of-donald-trumps-trade-wars.

Annie Lowrey, "Where Biden Agrees With Trump," *Atlantic*, October 5, 2021, https://www.theatlantic.com/ideas/archive/2021/10/why-bidens-china-trade-policy-remains-so-fraught/620244/.

Kris Maher, "In a Pennsylvania Steel Town, Donald Trump's Tariff Is a Winner," *Wall Street Journal*, March 3, 2018, https://www.wsj.com/articles/in-a-pennsylvania-steel-town-donald-trumps-tariff-is-a-winner-1520078400.

Ana Swanson, "In Washington, 'Free Trade' Is No Longer Gospel," *New York Times*, March 17, 2021, https://www.nytimes.com/2021/03/17/business/economy/free-trade-biden-tai.html.

Ana Swanson, "The U.S. trade deficit soared to a record last year.," *New York Times*, February 8, 2022, https://www.nytimes.com/2022/02/08/business/us-trade-deficit.html.

Jackie Wattles and Jethro Mullen, "Trump threatens China with new $100 billion tariff plan," CNN Money, April 6, 2018, https://money.cnn.com/2018/04/05/news/trump-tariff-china-trade-war/index.html.

Josh Zumbrun, "The $67 Billion Tariff Dodge That's Undermining U.S. Trade Policy," *Wall Street Journal*, April 25, 2022, https://www.wsj.com/articles/the-67-billion-tariff-dodge-thats-undermining-u-s-trade-policy-di-minimis-rule-customs-tourists-11650897161.

OPPOSING VIEWPOINTS® SERIES

CHAPTER 4

Is Globalization a Force for Good?

Chapter Preface

The end result of global trade is globalization, a term that refers to a political, cultural, and social landscape that exists primarily in relation to people who are geographically distant from it. This is a good thing as often as it's a bad one: it feels like you can talk to almost anyone in the world, instantaneously; it feels like almost anyone in the world can talk to you, whether you want them to or not.

Communication is the most literal form of globalization, but the small ways that the world has become globalized are just as stirring. Culture that was once confined to the borders of language and shared references now seemingly flows smoothly from streaming platforms to potential audiences anywhere. Parts of the world that were long considered abstract are now viewed in vivid detail.

But these transformations don't occur equally, and critics of globalization argue that the infusion of wealth that's brought about by these new marketplaces only exacerbates how unequally capital is distributed around the world. As the axiom goes: the rich get richer, and the poor get correspondingly poorer as the larger world becomes more polluted in order to fill the vast new demands of constantly connected consumers.

The viewpoints in this chapter look at both sides of this rhetorical divide. For the optimists, the potential of new solutions outweighs the anxiety of new problems. The biggest environmental problem of our time—climate change—can only be approached through global policy, they argue. It will do no good for the health of the planet if greenhouse gasses are only abandoned in the so-called developed half of the world. The consequences of these changes will be felt, on some level, around the world. The genie is out of the bottle. Globalization is essentially inescapable, and the real question to address is how a globalized world ought to work.

VIEWPOINT 1

> "Many countries have seen great prosperity thanks to the disintegration of trade regulations that had otherwise been considered a harbinger of free trade in the recent past."

The Long Story of Trade Liberalization

Raymon Huston and R. Adam Dastrup

In the following viewpoint Raymon Huston and R. Adam Dastrup argue that trade today is not substantially different than it was in the past. The most significant change is how efficiently trade is conducted. Efficiency has long been a goal of trade, stretching back to the origin of money, which the authors argue was created to make trade more efficient. As this viewpoint puts it, today's debates about trade policy are part of a larger story that seems far away from an ending. Raymon Huston is a Political Science professor at Tulsa Community College. Adam Dastrup is geography professor at Salt Lake Community College.

As you read, consider the following questions:

1. What is the difference between trade that happens directly between countries and the vast majority of what's called trade "between nations"?

"Globalization and International Trade," OPEN OKSTATE. https://open.library.okstate.edu/culturalgeography/chapter/7-5/. Licensed under CC BY-4.0 International.

2. What are some of the fundamental reasons that nations trade, according to the authors?
3. What kinds of products do countries with a relative abundance of low-skilled labor tend to specialize in?

Before we begin a discussion about why nations trade, it would be helpful to take a moment to consider the character and evolution of trade. It is important to keep in mind, first, that although we frequently talk about trade "between nations," the vast majority of international transactions today take place between private individuals and private enterprises based in different countries. Governments sometimes sell things to each other, or individuals or corporations in other countries, but these comprise only a small percentage of world trade.

Trade is not a modern invention. International trade today is not qualitatively different from the exchange of goods and services that people have been conducting for thousands of years. Before the widespread adoption of currency, people exchanged goods and some services through bartering—trading a certain quantity of one good or service for another good or service with the same estimated value. With the emergence of money, the exchange of goods and services became more efficient.

Developments in transportation and communication revolutionized economic exchange, not only increasing its volume but also widening its geographical range. As trade expanded in geographic scope, diversity, and quantity, the channels of trade also became more complex. Individuals conducted the earliest transactions in face-to-face encounters. Many domestic transactions, and some international ones, still follow that pattern. However, over time, the producers and the buyers of goods and services became more remote from each other.

A wide variety of market actors, individuals and firms, emerged to play supportive roles in commercial transactions. These "middlemen," wholesalers, providers of transportation services, providers of market information, and others, facilitate transactions that would be too complex, distant, time-consuming, or broad for individuals to conduct face-to-face efficiently.

International trade today differs from economic exchange conducted centuries ago in its speed, volume, geographic reach, complexity, and diversity. However, it has been going on for centuries, and its fundamental character, the exchange of goods and services for other goods and services or money, remains unchanged.

That brings us to the question of why nations trade. Nations trade a lot, but it is not quite as obvious why they do so. Put differently, why do private individuals and firms take the trouble of conducting business with people who live far away, speak different languages, and operate under different legal and economic systems, when they can trade with fellow citizens without having to overcome any of those obstacles?

It seems evident that if one country is better at producing one good and another country is better at producing a different good (assuming both countries demand both goods) that they should trade. What happens if one country is better at producing both goods? Should the two countries still trade? This question brings into play the theory of comparative advantage and opportunity costs.

The everyday choices that we make are, without exception, made at the expense of pursuing one or several other choices. When you decide what to wear, what to eat for dinner, or what to do on Saturday night, you are making a choice that denies you the opportunity to explore other options.

The same holds for individuals or companies producing goods and services. In economic terms, the amount of the good or service that is sacrificed to produce another good or service is known as opportunity cost. For example, suppose Switzerland can produce either one pound of cheese or two pounds of chocolate in an hour. If it chooses to produce a pound of cheese in a given hour, it forgoes the opportunity to produce two pounds of chocolate. The two pounds of chocolate, therefore, is the opportunity cost of producing the pound of cheese. They sacrificed two pounds of chocolate to make one pound of cheese.

A country is said to have a comparative advantage in whichever good has the lowest opportunity cost. That is, it has a comparative advantage in whichever good it sacrifices the least to produce. In the example above, Switzerland has a comparative advantage in the production of chocolate. By spending one hour producing two pounds of chocolate, it gives up producing one pound of cheese, whereas, if it spends that hour producing cheese, it gives up two pounds of chocolate.

Thus, the good in which comparative advantage is held is the good that the country produces most efficiently (for Switzerland, it is chocolate). Therefore, if given a choice between producing two goods (or services), a country will make the most efficient use of its resources by producing the good with the lowest opportunity cost, the good for which it holds the comparative advantage. The country can trade with other countries to get the goods it did not produce (Switzerland can buy cheese from someone else).

The concepts of opportunity cost and comparative advantage are tricky and best studied by example: consider a world in which only two countries exist (Italy and China) and only two goods exist (shirts and bicycles). The Chinese are very efficient in producing both goods. They can produce a shirt in one hour and a bicycle in two hours. The Italians, on the other hand, are not very productive at manufacturing either good. It takes three hours to produce one shirt and five hours to produce one bicycle.

The Chinese have a comparative advantage in shirt manufacturing, as they have the lowest opportunity cost (1/2 bicycle) in that good. Likewise, the Italians have a comparative advantage in bicycle manufacturing as they have the lowest opportunity cost (5/3 shirts) in that good. It follows, then, that the Chinese should specialize in the production of shirts and the Italians should specialize in the production of bicycles, as these are the goods that both are most efficient at producing. The two countries should then trade their surplus products for goods that they cannot produce as efficiently.

A comparative advantage not only affects the production decisions of trading nations, but it also affects the prices of the goods involved. After the trade, the world market price (the price an international consumer must pay to purchase a good) of both goods will fall between the opportunity costs of both countries. For example, the world price of a bicycle will be between 5/3 shirt and two shirts, thereby decreasing the price the Italians pay for a shirt while allowing the Italians to profit. The Chinese will pay less for a bicycle and the Italians less for a shirt than they would pay if the two countries were manufacturing both goods for themselves.

In reality, of course, trade specialization does not work precisely the way the theory of comparative advantage might suggest, for several reasons:

- No country specializes exclusively in the production and export of a single product or service.
- All countries produce at least some goods and services that other countries can produce more efficiently.
- A lower income country might, in theory, be able to produce a particular product more efficiently than the United States can but still not be able to identify American buyers or transport the item cheaply to the United States. As a result, U.S. firms continue to manufacture the product.

Generally, countries with a relative abundance of low-skilled labor will tend to specialize in the production and export of items for which low-skilled labor is the predominant cost component. Countries with a relative abundance of capital will tend to specialize in the production and export of items for which capital is the predominant component of cost.

Many American citizens do not fully support specialization and trade. They contend that imports inevitably replace domestically produced goods and services, thereby threatening the jobs of those involved in their production.

Is Globalization a Force for Good?

Imports can indeed undermine the employment of domestic workers. We will return to this subject a little later. From what you have just read, you can see that imports supply products that are either 1) unavailable in the domestic economy or 2) that domestic enterprises and workers would be better off not making so that they can focus on the specialization of another good or service.

Finally, international trade brings several other benefits to the average consumer. Competition from imports can enhance the efficiency and quality of domestically produced goods and services. Also, competition from imports has historically tended to restrain increases in domestic prices.

- Name a product/business where labor would be the comparative advantage for a developing country.
- Name a product/business where capital would be the comparative advantage for a rich country.
- Name a product/business where natural resources would be a comparative advantage.

Global Interdependence

The tremendous growth of international trade over the past several decades has been both a primary cause and effect of globalization. The volume of world trade increased twenty-seven-fold from $296 billion in 1950 to $8 trillion in 2005. Although international trade experienced a contraction of 12.2 percent in 2009, the steepest decline since World War II, trade is again on the upswing.

As a result of international trade, consumers around the world enjoy a broader selection of products than they would if they only had access to domestically made products. Also, in response to the ever-growing flow of goods, services, and capital, a whole host of U.S. government agencies and international institutions have been established to help manage these rapidly developing trends.

Although increased international trade has spurred tremendous economic growth across the globe, raising incomes, creating jobs, reducing prices, and increasing workers' earning power, trade can also bring about economic, political, and social disruption.

Since the global economy is so interconnected, when large economies suffer recessions, the effects are felt around the world. One of the hallmark characteristics of the global economy is the concept of interdependence. When trade decreases, jobs, and businesses are lost. In the same way that globalization can be a boon for international trade; it can also have devastating effects. Activities such as the choice of clothes you buy have a direct impact on the lives of people working in the nations that produce.

There are several elements that are responsible for the expansion of the global economy during the past several decades: new information technologies, reduction of transportation costs, the formation of economic blocs such as the North American Free Trade Association (NAFTA), and the reforms implemented by states and financial organizations in the 1980s aimed at liberalizing the world economy.

Trade liberalization, or deregulation, has become a "hot button" issue in world affairs. Many countries have seen great prosperity thanks to the disintegration of trade regulations that had otherwise been considered a harbinger of free trade in the recent past. The controversy surrounding the issue, however, stems from enormous inequality and social injustices that sometimes comes with reducing trade regulations in the name of a bustling global economy.

Given the dislocations and controversies, some people question the importance of efforts to liberalize trade and wonder whether the economic benefits are outweighed by other unquantifiable negative factors such as labor exploitation.

With globalization, competition occurs between nations having different standards for worker pay, health insurance, and labor regulations. Corporations benefit from lower labor costs found in developing regions, thanks to free-trade agreements and a new international division of labor. A worker in a high-wage country is thus increasingly struggling in the face of competition from workers in low-wage countries. Entire sectors of employment in developed countries are now subject to this growing international competition, and unemployment has crippled many localities.

The outcome has been an international division of labor in all sectors of the economy. In particular, manufacturing is increasingly being contracted out to lower-cost locations, which are often found in developing countries with no minimum wage and few environmental regulations.

An excellent example of international division of labor can be found in the clothes-making industry. What was once a staple industry in most developed Western economies has now been relocated to developing countries in Central America, Eastern Europe, North Africa, Asia, and elsewhere.

International Development Models

Self-Efficiency Model of Development

There are two models of economic development that play off each other as a way to. The first model is called the Self-Efficiency Model of Development, which encourages domestic development of goods and resources and discourages foreign influence and investment. Between 1990 to 2000, this was the primary form of economic development until globalization became the dominant force. What makes this model of development competitive to international trade models is that governments create barriers through the form of tariffs on imports, which makes them more expensive and less economically competitive with their local businesses. New businesses are nurtured until they and economically sustainable and competitive enough to compete with businesses abroad.

This model of development prides itself in an equal distribution of resources to a nation's people and businesses over foreign entities and investments. But there are several critics of this form of development because they argue that this model protects inefficient businesses and does not reward competitive and highly efficient ones, requires a sizeable bureaucratic government to administer this model of development and limit abuse and corruption, and does not receive the benefits of rewarding foreign corporations that could provide goods and services to countries with limited resources.

Modernization Model of Development

The other model for economic development is through international trade. W.W. Rostow proposed in the 1950s the idea of a five-stage model of development that competes with the self-sufficiency model. In a report by Peter Kasanda, Rostow's Modernization Theory of Development implies that nations should use local resources and industries to sell scarce or needed resources globally through international trade. The money that comes back to the country would increase the nation's GDP, which could then be used to improve the development of infrastructure, invest in education and healthcare, and ultimately improve a country's standard of living. The following is the 5-stage model of how progress and development might occur for a country:

Traditional Society—This primary sector is determined for societies that have little economic development and a high percentage of people active in family-scale subsistence agriculture. Most of the money for development goes toward religious or military activities.

Economic Growth—Key investments in core structures of an existing economy to expand its development. Structured invests in mining and large-scale agriculture and with technology to enhance the efficiency of existing infrastructure. The goal is to invest in the overall structure of the nation's economy, so the production of goods can begin to occur.

Economic Takeoff—Investment and development lead to expanded, but limited activity in mining, textile, and food production along with continued improvements and investment in modern technology. A key indicator of the "takeoff" stage is when the people in the country become more driven by economic development rather than traditional activities. Is should also be noted that this is often when concerning issues of slavery and sweatshops begin to surface if not appropriately handled.

Drive to Economic Maturity—During this period, society is driven by modern technological advances over most other areas of the economy. Technology drives production and efficiency throughout all parts of the economy. It is at this time when a local economy becomes an international economic player. This stage is often said to be an extension of the "takeoff" stage, but more expansive than limited in scope.

Age of Mass Consumption—This final stage of economic development occurs when an economy shifts from a secondary sector of manufacturing toward the tertiary sector of services. The economic status of the nation's society also becomes driven by mass consumption of disposable goods.

The theory of international trade has become the preferred way to improve economic development. The reason is that most nations cannot produce all the goods and resources they require. So if nations can focus on specific goods and services to export, they can return the purchase of the goods and services they need.

In 1995, the World Trade Organization (WTO) was created to represent 97 percent of the world-trading establishment. It is through the WTO that nations can negotiate with each other international trade restrictions, governmental subsidies, and tariffs on exports. The WTO also has the power to act as an international court to enforce international agreements.

Liberals and conservatives have highly attacked the WTO. Liberals believe that too many actions or rulings are done undemocratically and behind closed doors. They also believe the organization focuses more on the rights of corporations rather than poorer nations. Conservatives believe that no international organization has the right to dictate the choices of sovereign nations.

VIEWPOINT 2

> "Our economic model today is overly dependent on the unsustainable use of natural resources."

Facing Our Global Environmental Challenges Requires Efficient International Cooperation

Erik Lundberg

In this viewpoint, Erik Lundberg argues that global cooperation is vital to developing a public policy framework that can tackle the challenges of climate change, among other environmental issues. It is the very organizations that bring about a globalized world that also bring together leaders who can be convened to attend extensive meetings on these issues. What stands in the way of environmental policy is fragmentation between governments that have different goals, many of which aren't often reconcilable. But the environmental crisis is one that will impact everybody, eventually. Erik Lundberg is a Finnish ambassador and the country's representative to the United Nation's Environment Programme.

As you read, consider the following questions:

1. What big challenges are facing humankind around the world, according to the viewpoint?

"Facing Our Global Environmental Challenges Requires Efficient International Cooperation," by Erik Lundberg, United Nations Environment Programme (UNEP), July 4, 2019. Reprinted by permission. https://www.unep.org/news-and-stories/editorial/facing-our-global-environmental-challenges-requires-efficient.

2. How does this viewpoint relate global connectedness to looking at issues like climate change?
3. Why is fragmentation a major challenge for global environmental policy?

Our planet and humankind face three unprecedented, mutually reinforcing challenges: climate change, the loss of biodiversity and the overuse of critical natural resources.

In the past year, we have seen intense heatwaves and raging wildfires in Europe, the United States and in Japan cause huge economical loss and damage. In Africa and Asia, tropical cyclones and typhoons killed over a thousand people and devastated the lives of tens of millions more. In East Africa, droughts are getting more severe, the rains more intense. Somalia is at the edge of famine because of the drought.

We are also witnessing extreme loss of life in natural environments. In 2019, more than 27,000 species are threatened with extinction.

Our economic model today is overly dependent on the unsustainable use of natural resources. According to the United Nations, the extraction and processing of natural resources is the cause of half of global greenhouse gas emissions, and 80 to 90 per cent of biodiversity loss. Only nine per cent of man-made materials remain in circulation.

Time is running out. We need a coordinated, comprehensive and swift response to these challenges. We cannot continue with our traditional economic and consumption models. There is no planet B.

Finland Is Ready to Take Action, but No Country Can Achieve Sustainable Results on Their Own

Finland's new government has set the challenge of climate change as the starting point for its government programme. The ambitious, greenest ever government agenda aims to achieve carbon neutrality by 2035—becoming the first fossil-free welfare society in the world. Finland also aims to stop the loss of biodiversity and intensify efforts to transition into a circular economy. We are the first country in the world to incorporate the 2030 Agenda in our 2019 state budget, with resources allocated for carbon-neutrality and the smart use of natural resources, and the main taxes contributing to sustainable development. State budgeting is, in our view, a very powerful tool to implement the 2030 Agenda.

Finland also has strong cross-sectoral coordination mechanisms between different ministries as well as other environmental interest groups.

No country, however, can successfully meet these global challenges on their own. We need to work closely together to find comprehensive and effective solutions. We need to increase cooperation, both at the national and the international level. We need to involve civil society, academia, business and governments.

The U.N. Environment Assembly and the U.N. Environment Programme Can Become Even Stronger and More Effective

Finland has consistently called for the improvement of what we call the "international environmental governance." Previous, systematic reform efforts have aimed to improve coherence, coordination and effectiveness, with the Rio+20 meeting in 2012 as a key milestone. Reform efforts have focused specifically on 1) the governance, financing, and functioning of UN Environment, and 2) enhancement of synergies among multilateral environmental agreements.

The most significant reform so far has been the transformation of UN Environment's 58-member governing council into the universal UN Environment Assembly, bringing political leaders of all United Nations Member States to the same table to discuss our common environmental agenda. Despite its successes, the UN Environment Assembly is still a young United Nations body and needs further strengthening so that it can take its rightful place within the United Nations system.

As of today, the UN Environment Assembly takes decisions about the work of UN Environment. Instead, it should give strategic guidance to Member States and the international environmental governance system to increase political interest in the environmental agenda, and to motivate and ensure political action both within the United Nations and nationally.

At its fourth meeting in March 2019, the UN Environment Assembly decided to establish a Member State-led review process of its governing bodies, which will culminate in decisions at the Fifth UN Environment Assembly in 2021. We must use this process well and, in accordance with the decision taken at the Fourth Assembly, keep the broad vision of a strengthened UN Environment Assembly firmly in mind.

Finland will hold the Presidency of the European Council for six months as of 1 July 2019 and will be in a key position to coordinate the European Union's views on the review process.

Boosting the Environmental Voice and Agenda Within the United Nations System

We also need to discuss UN Environment's and the Assembly's role in the wider United Nations system, to bring the environment more firmly to the core of the United Nations. Linkages between the UN Environment Assembly and the governing bodies of other United Nations entities, the High-Level Political Forum as well as multilateral environmental agreements are crucial and need to be promoted in order to support the 2030 Agenda implementation.

Finland underlines UN Environment's role as the main environmental coordinating body of the United Nations, working with other United Nations agencies through the Environment Management Group, with members from 51 multilateral bodies.

The ongoing broader United Nations reform offers good opportunities to enhance collaboration with the United Nations at the national level and to decrease competition between United Nations agencies. This is particularly important for UN Environment, due to its limited in-country presence. We support ongoing efforts within UN Environment to actively participate in the implementation of the United Nations reform.

Fragmentation Versus Synergy

A key challenge for effective international environmental governance is fragmentation. We have a myriad of multilateral environmental agreements, different in membership, scope, governance structure and funding mechanisms. Finland has actively been trying to promote synergies between different multilateral environmental agreements. We also support clarifying the relationship between multilateral environmental agreements and the UN Environment Assembly.

A recent report on international environmental governance, financed by the Nordic Council of Ministers, recommends that multilateral environmental agreements and their governing bodies are given a more prominent role during the UN Environment Assembly. It also suggests exploring a further alignment of UN Environment's programme of work and the multilateral environmental agreements.

While fully respecting the mandates of each multilateral environmental agreement, future UN Environment Assemblies should approach the environmental agenda in a holistic manner, actively looking for possible synergies. The UN Environment Assembly would also benefit from greater incorporation of science into decision-making and systematic linkage with different environmental assessment mechanisms.

VIEWPOINT 3

> "Without international trade, consumers would have limited choices, and could be forced to purchase only domestic goods that may have been produced under lax environmental standards."

Globalization May Be Better for the Environment

Sylvanus Kwaku Afesorgbor and Binyam Afewerk Demena

In this viewpoint, Sylvanus Kwaku Afesorgbor and Binyam Afewerk Demena challenge the opinion that globalization has had a negative impact on environmental conditions in modern history. The expanding reach of supply chains have given consumers more choices, thus allowing consumers to choose products that are better for the environment, the authors argue. Not every economic race is necessarily a race to the bottom. In fact, recent history has shown some consumers even race to the top, preferring to buy more sustainably sourced products. Sylvanus Kwaku Afesorgbor is asssociate professor in the department of Food, Agricultural and Resource Economics at the University of Guelph, Ontario. Binyam Afewerk Demena is an empirical economist with expertise across economic disciplines focusing on development, environment, and health.

"Globalization May Actually Be Better for the Environment," by Sylvanus Kwaku Afesorgbor and Binyam Afewerk Demena, The Conversation, April 24, 2018. https://theconversation.com/globalization-may-actually-be-better-for-the-environment-95406. Licensed under CC BY-4.0 International.

As you read, consider the following questions:

1. What is the "race-to-the-bottom hypothesis" of how globalization operates?
2. How can the "technique effect" impact the environmental impact of globalization?
3. Economic sanctions have largely locked Iranian businesses from feeling the impact of globalization. How did that impact environmental standards in the country?

The increasing pace of globalization and how it affects the environment has been a major global concern. Although the research has been fraught with contrasting results, there are many who strongly believe that increased globalization has been harmful to the environment.

A large number of environmentalists who support this view base their arguments on the premise that globalization leads to an increase in global demand, resulting in increased production. This indirectly contributes to the exploitation of the environment and the depletion of natural resources.

Amid rising environmental concerns, an important question is whether deglobalization would have the opposite impact on the environment. Put differently, if globalization is harmful, then should we expect that the current deglobalization trend will be less harmful for the environment?

It's an important question to ask right now considering the mounting anti-globalization sentiments that have engulfed the Global North.

We have not only witnessed Brexit, the election of Donald Trump, the Belgian opposition to the trade agreement between the European Union and Canada in the recent past, but more recently, we have seen anti-globalization sentiments heating up even in the United States, once the strongest architect and proponent of globalization in the world.

This is resulting in uncertainty and a near stalemate for NAFTA, steel and aluminium tariff hikes and the potential trade war with China.

Is Globalization Bad for the Environment?

The adverse effect of globalization on the environment is supported by what's known as the race-to-the-bottom hypothesis. This school of thought argues that increased gains from globalization are achieved at the expense of the environment because more open economies adopt looser environmental standards.

Those who support this bleak view of globalization argue it creates global competition, resulting in a boost in economic activities that deplete the environment and its natural resources.

The increased economic activity leads to greater emissions of industrial pollutants and more environmental degradation. The pressure on international firms to remain competitive forces them to adopt cost-saving production techniques that can be environmentally harmful.

Deglobalization May Worsen Emissions

But in fact, deglobalization may not necessarily translate into reduced emissions of harmful gases such as CO_2, SO_2, NO_2, but could actually worsen it. Through what's known as the technique effect, we know globalization can trigger environmentally friendly technological innovations that can be transferred from countries with strict environmental regulations to pollution havens.

Globalization doesn't just entail the movement of manufactured goods, but also the transfer of intermediate, capital goods and technologies. That means multinational corporations with clean state-of-the-art technologies can transfer their green know-how to countries with low environmental standards.

It's widely recognized that multinational firms use cleaner types of energy than local firms, and therefore have more energy-efficient production processes. Deglobalization could mean these environmentally friendly technologies aren't passed on to countries that are trying to go green.

The rise of anti-globalization forces also means less specialization in sectors in which countries have comparative advantages.

This can create an inefficient allocation of resources that leads to the dissipation of scarce economic and natural resources. If every country has to produce to meet its domestic demand, in other words, it could result in duplication in production processes and therefore an increase in local emissions.

Iran Sanctions Backfire for the Environment

Since some countries have weaker environmental standards than others, this could possibly worsen global emissions.

A good example of this is Iran, which has been slapped with economic sanctions, making the country less integrated in the world economy. The result has been domestic production that's wreaked immense havoc on the environment. As result of import bans of crude oil, for example, Iran started refining its own crude oil that contains 10 times the level of pollutants of the oil it used to import.

Globalization has another benefit—it's been at the forefront of creating public awareness about labour and environmental standards through the platforms of international activities such as fair trade and eco labels.

The success of this environmental public awareness has resulted in consumer preferences evolving. Producers are therefore able to build their customer base by producing eco-friendly products.

Without international trade, consumers would have limited choices, and could be forced to purchase only domestic goods that may have been produced under lax environmental standards.

WTO and RTAs Help Protect the Environment

Globalization achieved through multilateral negotiations via the World Trade Organization has also demonstrated that although environmental protection is not part of the WTO's core mandate, it has spurred enthusiasm within its member countries for sustainable development and environmentally friendly trade policies.

There are several WTO trade-related measures that are compatible with environmental protection and sustainable use of natural resources. For instance, the green provisions of the WTO direct countries to protect human, animal or plant life and conserve their exhaustible natural resources.

Apart from the WTO, regional trade agreements, known as RTAs, are another feature of globalization that promote environmentally sustainable policies. As countries seek to join RTAs, they are also made to simultaneously embrace environmental cooperation agreements.

Many countries, including Canada and those in the European Union, have developed national policies that stipulate that prior to signing any trade agreement, environmental impact assessments must be carried out. That means that any country that signs trade agreements with those countries must also automatically sign environmental cooperation deals.

China Leading While the U.S. Lagging?

We've seen over the years how countries like China, once pollution havens, are making tremendous gains in reducing their emissions, especially after becoming more integrated into the world economy.

Because of the incentives to increase global market access for its products, China has moved from the position of one of the world's top polluters into a global leader spearheading the fight against climate change and pollution.

In 2017, China closed down tens of thousands of factories that were not complying with its environmental standards.

In contrast, we have seen a country like the U.S. slowly drifting away from the climate change fight in part because of the anti-globalization inclinations of Donald Trump. He pulled the U.S. out of the Paris Agreement on climate change in keeping with his anti-globalization rhetoric during the 2016 U.S. election campaign.

Through its America First Energy Plan, the Trump administration has outlined its preference for polluting industries, the use of fossil fuels and the revival of the coal industry. This signals that deglobalizing countries may drift away from sustainable development practices towards industrial policies that are devastating to the environment.

As countries restrict international trade, the environment is likely at risk.

Deglobalization isolates countries, making them less likely to be responsible for the environment. The gains associated with globalization, on the other hand, can be used as effective bargaining strategies or an incentive to demand environmental accountability from countries hoping to benefit from global trading systems.

VIEWPOINT 4

> "Globalization and technological change both pose great opportunities for the world economy...However, the by-product is an economy that has become increasingly divided into winners and losers from this process."

Does Globalization Breed Inequality?

William Hauk

In the following viewpoint William Hauks argues the effects of globalization can't be divided from its capacity to split societies between losers and winners. This isn't anything new, the author admits. Divisions like these have been the primarily complaint about capitalist society since the mid-1800s. The line Hauk takes, however, is that globalization has the tendency to exacerbate these divides. He connects this to the capacity of technological developments to completely change the quality of life of their users and create an immediate divide between those who have it and those who don't. William Hauk is an economics professor at the University of South Carolina.

As you read, consider the following questions:

1. Why is income inequality increasing around the world, according to the author?

"Globalization and Inequality: Sharing Wealth One of Society's Greatest Challenges," by William R. Hauk, The Globe Post, January 30, 2019. Reprinted by permission.

2. What is the connection between technological development and income inequality?
3. How does globalization contribute to region inequality, according to the viewpoint?

One thing that nearly all observers of the American economy (and other developed countries around the world) can agree on is that income inequality has increased considerably in recent decades. The top 1 percent of households in the U.S. earned less than 10 percent of the total national income in 1980 but now earn over 20 percent. Income gains among the richest 0.01 percent of households are even more dramatic. The wage premium from having a college degree has also increased significantly during the same time.

The specter of a dynamic economy where the average income grows while those within the middle to lower economic classes see their standard of living stagnate has caused an increased focus on income inequality.

However, the sources of this increasing inequality are considerably more disputed. Two phenomena, also prominent in the last few decades, are typically cited: globalization and technological change.

Why Is Inequality Increasing?

Globalization can increase wage inequality in a relatively rich country by increasing the imports of manufactured goods using predominantly low-skilled labor from developing countries. Conversely, it opens more opportunities for exports in high-tech firms that use more high-skilled labor. These two forces can widen the wage gap between high-skilled and low-skilled workers.

Technological change can also potentially increase wage inequality. Fewer secretaries, typists, or assembly-line workers are needed if computers and automation replace them in the production process. Conversely, newer technology can increase the demand for the services of, say, engineers who can service those machines.

While the two explanations are not mutually exclusive, for a long time, many economists tended to favor the technological explanation. If the trade was the stronger component of the story, then we would expect high-skill intensive industries to get bigger, while less-skill intensive industries got smaller. High-tech industries would expand as they serviced export markets. Older manufacturing industries, such as textiles, would disappear in the face of imports.

Changing Employment

While this story does explain some of what has happened to the U.S. economy, the evidence is that employment in the U.S. has changed more within sectors than across sectors. Instead of some sectors employing more workers while others employed less, each sector tended to change the composition of their workforce in the direction of more skilled workers. This observation is more consistent with the technological explanation than the globalization and trade explanation.

The policy implications are interesting. We may have some influence at the margin over globalization. Indeed, part of President Donald J. Trump's agenda, both as a candidate and in office, has been to negotiate "fairer" trade deals that would likely have the effect of decreasing international trade. Reducing the rate of technological development, however, is a policy choice that would strike most politicians as neither feasible nor desirable.

The analysis above views trade and technology as competing explanations of wage inequality. However, a line of research that has developed over the last decade suggests that they may, in fact, be complementary. Dating back to a model developed by economist Marc Melitz in 2003, recent research has focused on how trade may disproportionately benefit the most technologically advanced firms.

The upshot of this literature is that international trade presents more opportunities for the most productive firms in an industry. As trade barriers fall, high-productivity firms will be best positioned to take advantage of markets overseas. However, less-productive firms will likely be crowded out of an industry due to the expansion of their more productive competitors as well as imports. As a practical matter, "high-productivity" firms typically have disproportionately more high-skilled workers and high-tech capital than less productive firms.

Thus, while an industry does not necessarily need a change in its overall level of employment, exposure to international trade might change the composition of its employment. More trade tends to benefit the firms that employ the most high-skilled workers while hurting their less-skilled counterparts.

Regional Inequality

Also receiving attention in recent research is the extent to which some of these trade-induced changes can create regional inequality. Pioneering work by economists David Autor, David Dorn, and Gordon Hanson has shown that increased exposure to trade with China created large and persistent shocks to areas of the United States where import-competing firms were located.

In short, the relevant question does not seem to be whether globalization or technological change is increasing income inequality in the United States. They seem to be complementary, rather than competing explanations. The more important question is what policies, if any, might address this challenge.

Globalization and technological change both pose great opportunities for the world economy. Both have helped lead to historical reductions in global poverty. However, the by-product is an economy that has become increasingly divided into winners and losers from this process. How we share this wealth will be one of our greatest challenges as a society in the coming years.

VIEWPOINT 5

> "Wealth inequality is not only a problem within emerging and low-income nations—it is also increasing in the advanced economies."

Wealth Inequality Is Everyone's Problem
Market Business News

In this viewpoint, the writers at the website Market Business News take a more optimistic view of how globalization has impacted the world. Adjusted for inflation, for what it used to cost to buy a computer in 1960, you could buy 125 of them by 1990 and four times that number by 1998. This means more people can buy computers than ever before. Issues like wealth inequality, this viewpoint posits, exist everywhere and can perhaps be best solved together. Market Business News is a news website founded by Joseph and Christian Nordqvist.

As you read, consider the following questions:

1. How does this viewpoint define "economic globalization?"
2. What social improvements does this viewpoint attribute to the kinds of economic development associated with globalization?
3. What is this viewpoint's take on the question of whether or not globalization brings more inequality?

"What Is Economic Globalization?" Market Business News. Reprinted by permission.

Global Trade and the Supply Chain

Economic globalization refers to the mobility of people, capital, technology, goods and services internationally. It is also about how integrated countries are in the global economy. It refers to how interdependent different countries and regions have become across the world.

In the eighteen hundreds in the world economy generally, people and capital crossed borders with ease, but not goods. In this century, people do not cross borders easily, but technologies, capital and goods do.

Over the past two to three decades, under the framework of General Agreement on Tariffs and Trade (GATT) and World Trade Organization, economic globalization has been expanding at a much faster pace. Countries have rapidly been cutting down trade barriers and opening up their current accounts and capital accounts.

This rapid increase in pace has occurred mainly with advanced economies integrating with emerging ones. They have done this by means of foreign direct investment and some cross-border immigration. They have also reduced trade barriers.

In some regions of the world, such as the European Union, a large area almost the size of a continent has opened up to the free movement of capital, labor, goods and services. The North American Free Trade Agreement (NAFTA) opened up the free movement of goods and services, but not labor.

Cuba and North Korea are among the most autarkic (self-sufficient) and isolated nations on the planet. The two countries are the last bastions of the Soviet economic model.

Economic Globalization Linked to Greater Wealth and Inequality

While becoming more integrated into the global economy tends to bring increased wealth to a nation, globalization is commonly linked to greater inequality.

According to the United Nations:

> Economic globalization refers to the increasing interdependence of world economies as a result of the growing scale of cross-

border trade of commodities and services, flow of international capital and wide and rapid spread of technologies. It reflects the continuing expansion and mutual integration of market frontiers, and is an irreversible trend for the economic development in the whole world at the turn of the millennium.

Economic development, apart from GDP growth, also includes improvements in literacy, life expectancy, and people's well-being.

Can Global Culture Be More Sustainable?

Culture is a dynamic force for change rather than a rigid set of forms or parameters that must be strictly adhered to. As the World Commission on Culture and Development (WCCD) noted, a society's culture is neither static nor unchanging but rather is in a constant state of flux, influencing and being influenced by other world-views and expressive forms.

The current era of globalization, with its unprecedented acceleration and intensification in the global flows of capital, labour, and information, is having a homogenizing influence on local culture. While this phenomenon promotes the integration of societies and has provided millions of people with new opportunities, it may also bring with it a loss of uniqueness of local culture, which in turn can lead to loss of identity, exclusion and even conflict. This is especially true for traditional societies and communities, which are exposed to rapid "modernisation" based on models imported from outside and not adapted to their context.

Balancing the benefits of integrating into a globalized world against protecting the uniqueness of local culture requires a careful approach. Placing culture at the heart of development policies does not mean to confine and fix it in a conservative way, but on the contrary to invest in the potential of local resources, knowledge, skills and materials to foster creativity and sustainable progress. Recognition and respect for the diversity of cultures also creates the conditions for mutual understanding, dialogue and peace.

"Culture for Sustainable Development," published by the United Nations Educational, Scientific and Cultural Organization (UNESCO)

Global Trade and the Supply Chain

Advances in Science and Technology

The United Nations says the fast globalization of the world's economies over recent decades is mainly due to the rapid development of science and technologies. They have created an environment in which the market economic system can spread across frontiers.

For example, the Internet and electronic communications today mean that businesses can employ workers from virtually anywhere in the world, and can trade in several countries at the same time without having to physically open up branches there.

Thanks to scientific and technological progress, transportation and communication costs today are just a fraction of what they used to be. Compared to 1930, current shipping costs are today about 50% cheaper, airfreight costs are now just 1/6 of what they were 85 years ago, while communication costs are just 1% of what they were.

With what it used to cost to buy a computer in 1960 (in today's dollars), you could buy 125 of them by 1990, and four times that number by 1998. All these advances in science, technology and communications have helped drive economic globalization.

The Internet and electronic communications have allowed advanced economies to outsource many of their jobs offshore. In the US, Canada, and EU, millions of jobs have been transferred abroad. Call center positions, especially, have gone overseas. These jobs have gone mainly to India, the Caribbean, and other English-speaking emerging economies.

The economic systems that exist in the world today are much more complex than in ancient times, when humans survived by hunting and subsistence farming.

Globalization of the Automotive Industry

Today, the automotive industry has companies producing vehicle parts and then assembling them in several countries. Most current parts production, assembly and vehicle sales take place in integrated regions.

These car production regions include MERCOSUR in Latin America, ASEAN in Asia, and NAFTA in North America. They also include the European Union and CIS for the former Soviet Bloc countries.

Within those regions, certain countries stand out—in China, Brazil, Mexico, Russia and India, car production and assembly have increased dramatically over the past 20 years.

The city of Detroit in the United States is still synonymous with auto manufacturing. America's "Big Three," i.e., Ford, General Motors and Chrysler, are still based there. However, the expansion in those three companies' operations have occurred outside the city, and mainly abroad.

Patrice Hill wrote in the Washington Times in August 2013:

> The "Big Three" long ago moved some of the biggest chunks of their production, jobs and plants to places as near as Ohio and Ontario and as far away as China, Brazil and Russia. Without the plentiful factory jobs and incomes that once made Detroit a wealthy and teeming metropolis, the city steadily deteriorated into a hollow shell of vacant buildings and weed-covered lots. Last month, it became the largest American city ever to declare bankruptcy.

Does Globalization Bring More Inequality?

As the world has become more economically globalized, so has the income and wealth inequality within countries. Some people believe globalization is the cause—this has so far been difficult to prove.

They argue that if companies have access to the whole world market, and most of those companies are located in a few countries—the US, EU and Japan—they will suck money out of the whole world in much greater quantities than if they sold just within their own markets.

The counter-argument is that globalization brings well-paid jobs (compared to local pay rates) to emerging economies. A Ford factory worker in Mexico earns more and has better workplace conditions than he would as a farm laborer.

When looking at inequality between nations, however, globalization has coincided with more equality between the advanced and emerging economies. The rich countries today represent a smaller percentage of global GDP compared to twenty or thirty years ago.

Wealth inequality is not only a problem within emerging and low-income nations—it is also increasing in the advanced economies.

Janet Yellen, who heads the Federal Reserve System of the United States (America's central bank), said in a speech at the Conference on Economic Opportunity and Inequality at the Federal Reserve Bank of Boston in October 2013 that wealth inequality in the US has widened since 1990.

Ms. Yellen added that there are still opportunities in the country to bridge the wealth and income gap.

VIEWPOINT 6

> "Not only has globalization increased wealth and prosperity worldwide, it has produced a more peaceful world."

Global Trade Is the Way to Global Peace and Prosperity

Marco den Ouden

In the following viewpoint, Marco den Ouden argues that globalization encourages prosperity and peaceful relations among nations. The author cites data to support his argument that most regions around the world are much better off than they were 50 years ago. When centralized governments impose harsh trade restrictions, their people suffer and violence is more likely to ensue. Economic openness, on the other hand, tends to encourage peace. Marco den Ouden writes at The Jolly Libertarian.

As you read, consider the following questions:

1. What are the four "Tiger Economies," according to the viewpoint?
2. What is the theory of the Liberal Peace?
3. Why should libertarians support free trade, according to the author?

"Global Trade Is the Way to Global Peace and Prosperity," by Marco den Ouden, Foundation for Economic Education, February 13, 2018, https://fee.org/articles/global-trade-is-the-way-to-global-peace-and-prosperity/. Licensed under CC BY 4.0 International.

Capitalism is not nationalism. Capitalism knows no borders. Capitalism is not an exclusively American phenomenon. Free trade is the implementation of capitalism on an international basis.

Tiger Economies

In his marvellous book, *Eat the Rich*, P.J. O'Rourke points out that trade restrictions with that bastion of communism, Cuba, had, in fact, helped to entrench communism, not to erode it. A libertarian as well as a humorist, O'Rourke opines that the trade embargo gave "Castro an excuse for everything that's wrong with his rat-bag society. And free enterprise is supposed to be the antidote for socialism. We shouldn't forbid American companies from doing business in Cuba, we should force them to do so."

Much of the exportation of western ideals and western capitalism has taken over Asia. The four Tiger Economies, South Korea, Hong Kong, Taiwan and Singapore, are economic powerhouses and bastions of capitalism. O'Rourke explores Hong Kong in his book. He sees it as "the best contemporary example of laissez-faire" in the world.

He quotes John Cowperthwaite, the architect of the Hong Kong miracle who adopted a hands off approach to the economy: "... in the long run the aggregate of decisions of individual businessmen, exercising individual judgment in a free economy, even if often mistaken, is less likely to do harm than the centralized decisions of a government; and certainly the harm is likely to be counteracted faster."

These tiger economies spread and now include the Tiger Cubs—Indonesia, Malaysia, Thailand, Vietnam and the Philippines. The Wikipedia article on the Tiger Economies notes that "in Latin America, the fast-growing and emerging economies, oriented to free trade and free market development are called the Pacific Pumas which consist of Mexico, Chile, Peru & Colombia."

Economies adopting capitalism and free trade are emerging in Africa as well. This is all part of a policy of globalization—freeing up borders to the movement of goods and people with a minimum of government restriction.

Globalization Has Increased Prosperity

In his excellent book, *The Rational Optimist*, Matt Ridley details some of the triumphs of this policy, not just for the world but for the west as well. The first chapter, "A Better Today: The Unprecedented Present" should be mandatory reading for every doom and gloom soothsayer out there of whatever stripe. Ridley chronicles the incredible increase in prosperity for everyone that has resulted from international capitalism and free trade.

One sub-section is called "The Declaration of Interdependence." In it he argues that "self-sufficiency is not the route to prosperity." He points out that trade enables us to improve our wealth through the division of labor and specialization. He cites Leonard Read's classic essay "I, Pencil" which shows how an item as lowly as a pencil results from the input of many people from around the world, all brought together by the invisible hand that Adam Smith wrote about.

Ridley lays out some statistics that are truly astounding.

It is hard to find any region that was worse off in 2005 than in 1955," he writes. "The average South Korean lives twenty-six more years and earns fifteen times as much income each year as he did in 1955 (and earns fifteen times as much as his North Korean counterpart). The average Mexican lives longer now than the average Briton did in 1955. The average Botswanan earns more than the average Finn did in 1955. Infant mortality is lower in Nepal than it was in Italy in 1951. The proportion of Vietnamese living on less than $2 a day has dropped from 90 percent to 30 percent in twenty years.

The rich have got richer but the poor have done even better. The poor in the developing world grew their consumption twice as fast as the world as a whole between 1980 and 2000. The Chinese are ten times as rich, one-third as fecund and twenty-eight years longer-lived than they were fifty years ago. Even Nigerians are twice as rich, 25 percent less fecund and nine years longer-lived than they were in 1955. Despite a doubling of the world population, even the raw number of people living in absolute poverty (defined as less than a 1985 dollar a day) has fallen since the 1950s.

He notes that according to the United Nations, "poverty was reduced more in the last fifty years than in the previous 500."

Not only has globalization increased wealth and prosperity worldwide, it has produced a more peaceful world. That may seem an incredible claim considering continuing wars in places like Syria and parts of Africa, but it is true.

Unprecedented Peace

In his monumental book, *The Better Angels of Our Nature: Why Violence Has Declined*, Steven Pinker describes the steady decline of violence over the centuries, a trend that continues to this day, despite blips like the World Wars which he considers anomalies. He writes about the Rights Revolutions—civil rights, women's rights, children's rights, gay rights. He writes about the reduction in infanticide and child abuse, the effective end of lynchings, the steady decrease in violence towards gays and the increased awareness of spousal abuse and its reduction as a result.

And he writes about the Long Peace. Since 1945 we have entered an unprecedented period of peace. He presents a detailed argument complete with statistics to support his thesis. He looks for an explanation. The increase in the number of stable democracies is a factor. But an even larger factor is what he calls the Liberal Peace.

"The Democratic Peace," he writes, "is sometimes considered a special case of a Liberal Peace—"liberal" in the sense of classical liberalism, with its emphasis on political and economic freedom, rather than left-liberalism. The theory of the Liberal Peace embraces as well the doctrine of gentle commerce, according to which trade is a form of reciprocal altruism which offers positive-sum benefits for both parties and gives a selfish stake in the well-being of the other."

Pinker specifically mentions globalization, noting that "history suggests many examples in which freer trade correlates with greater peace." He cites the research of Bruce Russett and John Oneal. "They found that countries that depended more on trade in a given year were less likely to have a militarized dispute in the subsequent year."

"Russett and Oneal," he continues, "found it was not just the level of bilateral trade between nations in a pair that contributed to peace, but the dependence of each country on trade across the board: a country that is open to the global economy is less likely to find itself in a militarized dispute."

Some political scientists, he writes, have taken these findings "to entertain a heretical idea called the Capitalist Peace. The word liberal in Liberal Peace refers both to the political openness of democracy and to the economic openness of capitalism, and according to the Capitalist Peace heresy, it's the economic openness that does most of the pacifying."

Pinker concludes the section on the Liberal Peace with a quote from peace researcher Nils Petter Gleditsch who updated a popular 1960s anti-Vietnam War slogan to "Make money, not war!"

Libertarians have and should continue to support a policy of exporting liberal values of individual rights, peace, capitalism, and free trade to the world at large. If people are trapped in an insular state that oppresses its people, the ability to leave and seek freedom and opportunity elsewhere is the most precious of all rights. Given the opportunity, people will naturally gravitate toward freedom and prosperity. Globalization encourages this natural inclination as well as puts pressures on governments to liberalize their economies and to improve individual rights.

Periodical and Internet Sources Bibliography

The following articles have been selected to supplement the diverse views presented in this chapter.

Spencer Bokat-Lindell, "Do We Need to Shrink the Economy to Stop Climate Change?," *New York Times*, September 16, 2021, https://www.nytimes.com/2021/09/16/opinion/degrowth-cllimate-change.html.

David Brooks, "Globalization Is Over. The Global Culture Wars Have Begun," *New York Times*, April 8, 2022, https://www.nytimes.com/2022/04/08/opinion/globalization-global-culture-war.html

Peter Coy, "Globalization Isn't Over. It's Changing," *New York Times*, April 11, 2022, https://www.nytimes.com/2022/04/11/opinion/globalization.html.

Enda Curran, "Inflation, supply chains, COVID: The global economy has a lot of worries," *Los Angeles Times*, October 3, 2021, https://www.latimes.com/business/story/2021-10-03/global-economy-covid-final-quarter-2021.

Holly Ellyatt, Supply chain chaos is already hitting global growth. And it's about to get worse," CNBC, October 18 2021, https://www.cnbc.com/2021/10/18/supply-chain-chaos-is-hitting-global-growth-and-could-get-worse.html.

"Globalisation and autocracy are locked together. For how much longer?," *Economist*, March 19 2022, https://www.economist.com/finance-and-economics/2022/03/19/globalisation-and-autocracy-are-locked-together-for-how-much-longer.

Zeke Hausfather, "Absolute Decoupling of Economic Growth and Emissions in 32 Countries," The Breakthrough Institute, April 6, 2021, https://thebreakthrough.org/issues/energy/absolute-decoupling-of-economic-growth-and-emissions-in-32-countries.

Eric Levitz, "Only the Left Can Save Globalization Now," *New York Magazine*, February 9, 2021, https://nymag.com/intelligencer/2021/02/only-the-left-can-save-globalization-now.html.

John Micklethwait and Adrian Wooldridge, "Putin and Xi Exposed the Great Illusion of Capitalism," *Bloomberg*, March 24, 2022, bloomberg.com/opinion/articles/2022-03-24/ukraine-war-has-russia-s-putin-xi-jinping-exposing-capitalism-s-great-illusion?sref=B3uFyqJT.

Kelsey Piper, "Can we save the planet by shrinking the economy?," Vox, August 3, 2021, https://www.vox.com/future-perfect/22408556/save-planet-shrink-economy-degrowth.

Kenneth P. Pucker, "The Myth of Sustainable Fashion," *Harvard Business Review*, January 13, 2022, https://hbr.org/2022/01/the-myth-of-sustainable-fashion.

David Roberts, "Human success at the expense of other species is 'a pretty awful legacy,'" Vox, October 12, 2017, https://www.vox.com/energy-and-environment/2017/10/11/16457432/elizabeth-kolbert-biodiversity.

For Further Discussion

Chapter 1
1. What effects will disruptions to the supply chain have on various sectors around the world?
2. Will the unpopularity of globalization have any real political or economic impact? Why or why not?
3. Do you agree that supply chain sustainability is ultimately a very complex issue?

Chapter 2
1. Some experts have argued that computers laid the bedrock of the logistical revolution of the 1990s. How do you think the modern world would have developed differently without computers?
2. Do you think that export restrictions would only exacerbate hunger in parts of the world that rely on exports to provide essential food? Why or why not?
3. How can globalization be beneficial for the natural environment?

Chapter 3
1. Why are even educated voters uneducated about tariffs and quotas? How can that be changed?
2. What impact does trade have on economic growth?
3. Some companies use antiquated tax systems to lower the amount they pay in taxes. What could that revenue be used to fund instead?

Chapter 4

1. Is a global governing body realistic? What would be the benefits? What would be the drawbacks?
2. Do you think globalization is to blame for the widening wealth gap? Explain.
3. Are there environmental problems that are exacerbated by globalization that can be resolved by globally managed solutions? What are they?

Organizations to Contact

The editors have compiled the following list of organizations concerned with the issues debated in this book. The descriptions are derived from materials provided by the organizations. All have publications or information available for interested readers. The list was compiled on the date of publication of the present volume; the information provided here may change. Be aware that many organizations take several weeks or longer to respond to inquiries, so allow as much time as possible.

Asian Development Bank

6 ADB Avenue
Mandaluyong City 1550
Metro Manila, Philippines
+63 2 86324444
email: kkawamata@adb.org
website: www.adb.org

The Asian Development Bank is a regional banking group based in the Philippines that uses loans to facilitate development goals that the banks have in the region. The group is funded by bond issues as well as by the governments like the United States and Japan.

Association for Supply Chain Management

8430 W. Bryn Mawr Avenue Suite 1000
Chicago, IL 60631, USA
(773) 867-1777
email: support@ascm.org
website: www.ascm.org

This association calls itself the world's largest supply management association, "as well as one of the most respected." It was created in 1957 as the American Production and Inventory Control Society and later merged with the Supply-Chain Council in 2014. A year

Association for the Taxation of Financial Transactions and for Citizens' Action

66-72 rue Marceau 93
100 Montreuil-sous-bois France
France
website: www.attac.org/en

This group is singularly devoted to the issue of taxing foreign exchange transactions, which is where trade is conducted in a more abstract sort of way. According to the association, this will pave the way for "social, environmental and democratic alternatives in the globalisation process."

Beehive Design Collective

1 Elm Street
Machias, ME 04654
(207) 669-4117
email: pollinators@beehivecollective.org
website: www.beehivecollective.org

A local volunteer-led group of Maine designers, these people focus their attention on raising money to fund making posters that, according to one local newspaper attack "globalization in the Americas." Other relevant causes the group has made artwork opposing include "free trade, mountaintop removal coal mining [and] biotechnology."

Cato Institute

1000 Massachusetts Ave, NW
Washington, DC 20001
202–789-5200
email: pr@cato.org
website: cato.org/international

The Cato Institute in a right-wing think tank that was founded by one of the owners of Koch Industries, itself one of the largest companies in the world. According to the group, it advances polices that maintain that the United States "should thus engage the world, trade freely, and work with other countries on common concerns, but avoid trying to dominate the globe militarily."

Center for Strategic and International Studies

1616 Rhode Island Avenue, NW
Washington, DC 20036
202-887-0200
email: aschwartz@csis.org
website: www.csis.org

The center is a think tank that works in the foreign policy space. Among the topics that the group writes policy on are international development and global economics.

Centre for Economic Policy Research

33 Great Sutton Street, 2nd Floor
London EC1V 0DX
+44 (0)20 7183 8801
email: cepr@cepr.org
website: www.cepr.org

An organization with offices in Washington, D.C., Paris and London, this group hires economists to publish papers on the global economy. They also publish their findings in a more digestible form on their blog, voxeu.org.

Centre for the Study of Globalisation and Regionalisation

University of Warwick
Coventry, CV4 7AL
+44 (0)24 7652 3523
email: csgr@warwick.ac.uk
website: www.warwick.ac.uk/fac/soc/pais/research/csgr/

Funded the U.K. government's Economic and Social Research Council, this department of the University of Warwick tasks itself with studying "global (dis-)order." Recent research topics at the department include "Markets as Spectacles? Globalising Islamic Economies" and "European Leadership in Cultural, Science and Innovation Diplomacy."

The Council of Supply Chain Management Professionals

333 Butterfield Rd STE 140
Lombard, IL 60148
(630) 574-0985
email: msbaxa@cscmp.org
website: www.cscmp.org

This council dates to 1963 and says its goal is to "advance the supply chain profession." In addition to working to create a greater awareness of supply chains, the group also publishes various supply chain industry magazines like *Supply Chain Quarterly*, the *Journal of Business Logistics* and puts out an annual "State of Supply Chain Sustainability" report.

Global Trade Watch

215 Pennsylvania Ave, SE
Washington DC, 20003
(202) 454-5107
email: mstlouis@citizen.org
website: www.citizen.org

Run by Ralph Nader's former think tank Public Citizen, this group does work that reflects a more mildly left-wing take on the issue of globalization. According to its site, their angle is "to ensure that in this era of globalization, a majority have the opportunity to enjoy economic security, a clean environment, safe food, medicines and products."

International Finance Corporation

2121 Pennsylvania Avenue NW
Washington, DC 20433
(202) 473-1000
email: FMayer@ifc.org
website: www.ifc.org

The International Finance Corporation is a group that's run by the finance minsters of 185 countries, who pool money in order to invest it in projects that leaders there want to see in the world. The organization dates to the 1950s.

International Monetary Fund

700 19th Street, N.W.
Washington, D.C. 20431
email: publicaffairs_imf.org
website: www.imf.org

The International Monetary Fund (IMF) works to achieve sustainable growth and prosperity for all of its 190 member countries. It does so by supporting economic policies that promote financial stability and monetary cooperation, which are essential to increase productivity, job creation, and economic well-being. The IMF is governed by and accountable to its member countries.

Peterson Institute for International Economics

1750 Massachusetts Avenue
NW Washington, DC 20036-1903
202.328.9000
email: comments@piie.com
website: www.piie.com

The Peterson Institute is a think tank that generates polices the group says are "dedicated to strengthening prosperity and human welfare in the global economy through expert analysis." Among its stated goals is: "truth telling about the benefits of globalization and the costs of closed economies."

Bibliography of Books

Maxine Bédat. *Unraveled: The Life and Death of a Garment.* New York, NY: Penguin Random House, 2021.

Dan Breznitz. *Innovation in Real Places: Strategies for Prosperity in an Unforgiving World.* Oxford, U.K.: Oxford University Press, 2021.

Tom Burgis. *Kleptopia*. New York, NY: HarperCollins Books, 2020.

Annette Aurelie Desmarais. *La Via Campesina: Globalization and the Power of Peasants.* London, UK: Pluto Press, 2007.

Sally Eaves. *The Edge of Disruption: Ride the Wave of Digital Transformation.* London, U.K: Kogan Page, 2019.

Thomas Friedman. *Thank You for Being Late: An Optimist's Guide to Thriving in the Age of Accelerations.* New York, NY: Farrar, Straus and Giroux, 2016.

Harold James. *The War of Words: A Glossary of Globalization.* New Haven, CT: Yale University Press, 2021.

Stephen D. King. *Grave New World: The End of Globalization, the Return of History.* New Haven, CT: Yale University Press, 2017

Matthew C. Klein, Michael Pettis. *Trade Wars Are Class Wars: How Rising Inequality Distorts the Global Economy and Threatens International Peace.* New Haven, CT: Yale University Press, 2020.

Michael O'Sullivan. *The Levelling: What's Next After Globalization.* New York, NY: PublicAffairs, 2019

Paul Polman, Andrew Winston. *How Courageous Companies Thrive by Giving More Than They Take.* Cambridge, MA: Harvard Business Review Press, 2021.

Raghuram Rajan, *The Third Pillar*. New York, NY: Penguin Publishing Group, 2019.

Or Rosenboim. *The Emergence of Globalism: Visions of World Order in Britain and the United States, 1939–1950.* Princeton, NJ: Princeton University Press, 2017.

Suman Sarkar. *The Supply Chain Revolution: Innovative Sourcing and Logistics for a Fiercely Competitive World.* New York, NY: HarperCollins, 2017.

Donald Sassoon. *The Anxious Triumph: A Global History of Capitalism, 1860-1914.* New York, NY: Penguin, 2019.

Jason Schenker. *The Future After COVID: Futurist Expectations for Changes, Challenges, and Opportunities After the COVID-19 Pandemic.* Austin, TX: Prestige Professional Publishing, 2020.

Linda Scott. *The Double X Economy: The Epic Potential of Women's Empowerment.* New York, NY: Farrar, Straus and Giroux, 2020.

Murillo Xavier. *Advanced Strategies in Supply Chain: Competing in the New Normal.* Self-published, 2020.

Index

A

Advanced electronics, 23

Aerospace, 21, 37

Afesorgbor, Sylvanus Kwaku, 139-144

Afghanistan, 90, 92, 94-95, 99

Air transport, 37, 152

Albrecht, Brian C., 109-112, 114

Alicke, Knut, 19-25

Alliances, 87-104

Amazon, 51-52

American Chemistry Council (ACC), 83-84

American Petroleum Institute (API), 82

Analytics, 22-23

Asian Infrastructure Investment Bank, 65

Association of Southeast Asian Nations (ASEAN), 153

Australia, 80, 102

Automotive industry, 21, 23, 27-28, 37, 152

B

Balkans, 101

Bangladesh, 76-77, 111

Barriball, Ed, 19-25

Belarus, 38

Belgium, 140

Belts and Roads initiative, 38, 102

Biden, Joe, 36, 45, 61-62

Block, Walter, 59-62

Braneck, Dave, 44-52

Brazil, 153

Bretton-Woods, 66, 89

Brexit, 29, 64, 140

Bullwhip effect, 27, 29

C

Canada, 37, 140, 143, 152

Capitalism, 45-52, 60, 62, 156, 159

Central planning, 32-34

Chile, 156

China, 29, 32, 34, 37-38, 45-46, 49, 65, 79-81, 83-84, 91, 102-103, 141, 143, 148, 153

Climate change, 123, 135, 143

Cold War, 89-91, 93-94

Colombia, 113, 156

Commodities, 21, 23

Communism, 60, 89, 97, 156

Congress (U.S.), 113

Construction, 21, 23

COVID-19

  adaptation to, 20-25, 30, 49, 52

  Delta variant, 46

  health, 57

  lockdown, 20, 27, 29, 32, 46, 54, 56, 62

  Omicron variant, 29

  shut borders, 17, 20, 54

supply impact, 36, 37, 45-46, 49-50, 54, 58
vaccine, 27
Crimean Peninsula, 91, 102
Cuba, 150, 156

D

Dai, Tinglong, 35-39
Dastrup, R. Adam, 124-133
Debt shifting, 117
Defense Department (DOD), 90, 99
Defense industry, 21
Demand, 17, 20, 27-29, 43, 46, 48-49, 54
Demena, Binyam Afewerk, 139-144
Director of National Intelligence, 102
Distribution, 43, 48, 52

E

East Germany, 60-62
Economist, 78-85
End-to-end supply chain (E2E), 23
Energy, 27, 36, 46, 79, 82, 142, 144
Engineering industry, 21
Environment, 39, 54-55, 58, 73, 123, 131, 134-138, 140-144
European Deterrence Initiative (EDI), 92
European Union, 37-38, 71, 79, 102, 140, 143, 150, 152-153
  European Council, 137

F

Farand, Chloé, 53-55, 57-58
Farmers for Free Trade, 79
Federal Reserve, 154
Finland, 135-138
Food
  costs, 55
  crops, 37, 43, 54, 61-62
  famine, 36, 55
  grocery shelves, 60-61
  hunger, 54-57
  waste, 55-56, 58
Food and Agriculture Organization (FAO), 57
Food and Land Use Coalition, 58
Foreign direct investment (FDI), 116, 150
Free market/enterprise, 34, 60-62, 113, 156

G

General Agreement on Tariffs and Trade (GATT), 150
Germany, 60-62
Globalization, 30, 63-66, 71, 83, 116-119, 123-159
Great Resignation, 46-47
Greece, 82, 95
Group of 20 (G20), 80

H

Hauk, William, 145-148
Healthcare, 21, 23, 57
Hoarding, 27-28, 46

Index

Hong Kong, 156
Hungary, 64
Huston, Raymon, 124-133

I

Immigration, 29, 150
Income inequality, 146, 150-151, 153-154
Independent contractors, 48, 51
India, 65, 83, 111, 153
Indonesia, 114, 156
Infrastructure, 21, 79, 132
International Food Policy Research Institute, 55
International Monetary Fund, 89, 96, 116
International Trade Organization, 66
Inventory, 20, 24, 30
Iran, 43, 90-91, 98, 142
Iraq, 90, 92, 101
Irwin, Douglas, 74, 110-112, 114
Israel, 94
Italy, 102

J

Japan, 96, 100, 135, 153
Just-in-time manufacturing, 29-30, 48, 51

K

Kalibata, Agnes, 54-55, 57-58
Kanellos, Nikolaos Valantasis, 26-30

L

Labor
   shortage, 28-29, 46-49, 62
   trade, 74-76, 84, 128, 146
   unions, 50-52, 83
   working conditions, 29, 46-48, 130, 142
Layoffs, 17-18, 28
Libya, 101
Limbaugh, Rob, 84-85
Localizing supply, 20-21
Logistics, 17, 23, 43, 46-52, 56
Long Beach, California, 45, 49
Los Angeles, California, 45, 49
Lundberg, Erik, 134-138

M

Malaysia, 156
Manufacturing, 32, 43, 49, 51, 80, 84, 131
Market Business News, 149-154
Marshall Plan, 89
McDonald, Brad, 72-77
McInnis, Kathleen, 86-108
Medhora, Rohinton, 63-66
MERCOSUR (Southern Common Market), 153
Mexico, 49, 113, 153-154, 156
Modernization Theory of Development, 132

N

National Bureau of Economic Research, 80

173

National Defense Strategy Commission, 99
Nationalism, 65
Natural resources, 135-136, 141-143
Nearshoring, 21
Netherlands, 45
Network modeling, 24
Newark, New Jersey, 45
Nordic Council of Ministers, 138
North American Free Trade Agreement, 130, 141, 150, 153
North Atlantic Treaty Organization (NATO), 88-89, 92-97, 100-102
North Korea, 90-91, 150

O

Oakland, California, 49
Online shopping, 17, 43
Operation Iraqi Freedom, 101
Organization for Economic Cooperation and Development (OECD), 50, 119
Organization for Security and Cooperation in Europe, 94
Ouden, Marco den, 155-159
Outsourcing, 29, 43, 84, 131, 152
Oversupply, 27, 29

P

Palanský, Miroslav, 115-119
Panama, 113
Paris Agreement, 143
Peru, 156

Philippines, 64, 156
Populism, 64
Port congestion, 28, 32, 37, 45-46, 60
Portugal, 88
Production
  goods, 33, 37, 46, 49, 74, 126-128
  labor, 28, 47-48
  local, 21, 30
  offshore, 29-30

R

Race-to-the-bottom hypothesis, 141
Rail transport, 37, 51
Read, Leonard, 33, 157-158
Regional Comprehensive Economic Partnership, 65
Regulation, 39, 43, 48, 62
Remote work, 22
Ricardo, David, 73-74
Risk management, 21-22, 24
Russ, Katheryn, 80-81
Russia, 36-39, 65, 91, 98, 100, 102-103, 153
Rwanda, 54

S

SA Harvest, 56
Sanchez, Dan, 31-34
Savannah, Georgia, 45
Schiffling, Sarah, 26-30
Self-Efficiency Model of Development, 131

Index

Semiconductor chips, 22, 27-28, 37, 39
September 11 attacks, 90, 92, 98-99
Shipping
  containers, 17, 28, 45-46, 48, 50, 60
  costs, 28, 46, 152
  labor, 51
  logjams, 30, 32, 45, 50
  technology, 43
Shortages, 29, 32, 36, 46, 56, 60
Silk Road Initiative, 65
Singapore, 156
Smith, Adam, 34, 61, 73, 157
Somalia, 101
South Africa, 56
South Korea, 94, 100-101, 113, 156
Spain, 88
Sri Lanka, 111
Strategic transfer pricing, 117
Supply-chain tiers, 22, 27, 29
Supply base, 20-21
Syria, 90, 92, 101, 158

T

Taiwan, 49, 156
Tanzania, 37
Tariffs, 66, 71, 75, 77, 79-85, 111-114, 131, 141
Tax Foundation, 81
Tax havens, 116-119
Technology
  investment, 23-24
  labor, 24, 146-147
  logistics, 23, 56, 152
  transportation, 43
Thailand, 156
Tiger economies, 156-157
Trade
  agreements, 71, 77, 113, 140, 143, 147
  comparative advantage, 74, 126-129
  free, 73, 75, 87, 113, 130, 157
  history, 125-126
  opportunity cost, 126-128
  policy, 71, 76, 80, 110-112, 114, 156
  quotas, 79-80, 82
  regulation, 130
  war, 79-80, 82, 85, 96
Trautwein, Vera, 19-25
Treaty of Tordesillas, 88
Trucking, 29, 32, 47, 51, 62
Trump, Donald, 62, 64, 140, 143-144, 147
Turkey, 95

U

UCLA Sustainability Committee, 33
Ukraine, 36-39, 91
Unemployment, 45, 56, 62, 79-80, 131
Unitary model of taxation, 118
United Kingdom, 29, 45, 64, 66, 100
United Nations, 54, 88, 135, 150-152, 158

U.N. Conference on Trade and
    Development (UNCTAD), 55
U.N. Environment Program,
    136-138
U.N. Security Council, 94, 96
U.N. World Commission on
    Culture and Development
    (WCCD), 151
U.N. World Commission
    on Environment and
    Development, 33
United States, 36-38, 43, 46-47,
    49-52, 62, 64, 66, 75-77, 88-103,
    135, 140, 143, 146, 152-153, 156

V

Venezuela, 61
Vietnam, 28, 46, 101, 156

W

Walmart, 51, 52
Warsaw Pact, 94
West Germany, 60-62
World Bank, 77, 89, 96, 112
World Food Program (WFP), 55
World Trade Organization, 66, 77,
    133, 142-143, 150
World War II, 60-61, 76, 83, 87-89,
    92-93, 97, 102, 129

Y

Yemen, 55